KINGDOM

Kingdom Stewardship

Politics

Kennedy Vanterpool

Copyright © 2025 By Kennedy Vanterpool
All rights reserved

KINGDOM STEWARDSHIP SERIES
Kingdom Stewardship - Politics

Published by Prosperity Publishing Press
a division of Prosperity Ministry
16414 Lost Quail Dr, Missouri City, TX 77489

All rights reserved. No part of this book may be reproduced, stored in a retrieval system, or transmitted in any for—electronic, mechanical, photocopy, recording or any other—except brief quotes in printed reviews, without the prior written permission of the publisher.

Unless otherwise indicated, Scripture quotations are taken from the King James Version (KJV) Copyright 1988 by the
B. B. KIRKBRIDGE BIBLE COMPANY, INC.

Book Design: Jim Bisakowski, www.bookdesign.ca

ISBN: 978-1-952445-14-9
Published by Prosperity Publishing Press

prosperityministry.com

CONTENTS

	Introduction	5
Chapter 1	Why Do You Have Difficulty With Politics?	9
Chapter 2	The Kingdom And Politics	17
Chapter 3	A Biblical View of Politics	27
Chapter 4	Confusion Over Church and Politics	37
Chapter 5	Separation of Church and State: A Misnomer	45
Chapter 6	The Role of Pastors, Prophets, Priests, and Ministers	55
Chapter 7	Jesus and Politics	66
Chapter 8	Biblical Characters Involved in Politics	77
Chapter 9	Women and Politics	85
Chapter 10	The Bible is God's Manifesto and Constitution	93
Chapter 11	My Experience in Politics	99

Other Books by Kennedy Vanterpool include:

1. "You Are Prosperous, Believe It Or Not! My Personal Testimony"
2. "Some Things We Don't Have To Ask God For! Because He Is Our Father"
3. "The Great Disconnection! Between The Christian in Church and in Life! How to Solve It?
4. "Relationships 101, From Birth to Eternity"
5. "Why Are We So Afraid Of Changes? Understanding the Process"
6. "Understanding Discipleship! A Biblical Perspective"
7. "God Created You For Greatness! Are You Experiencing It?"
8. "Why Are So Many Christians Miserable! How to Avoid It"
9. "God's University! The School Everyone Must Attend"
10. "Congratulations! You Are A Member. Now What?"
11. "What Church Members Should Know About Cancer?"
12. "We Were Made To Worship God 24/7! Is It Possible?"
13. "We Are All Foreigners. This Is Not The World God Created You To Live In"
14. "Kingdom Living, How to Live Daily as the King You Are!"
15. "What Is Life About? It is Simpler Than You Think"
16. "Kingdom Stewardship: The Introduction"
17. "Kingdom Stewardship: The Titles"
18. "Kingdom Stewardship: Women"
19. "Kingdom Stewardship: Grief"
20. "Kingdom Stewardship: Relationship or Fellowship"
21. "Kingdom Stewardship: Suffering"
22. "Kingdom Stewardship: Prayer"
23. "Kingdom Stewardship: Love"
24. "It Is Possible To Worship God 24/7"
25. "How to Turn Your Grief into a Vibrant Ministry: A Practical, Easy-to-Use Manual"
26. "What is Life About? It is Simpler Than You Think"

Introduction

I thought that this manuscript was completed on July 2, 2018, and was ready to be sent to my layout personnel. I had forgotten about it for seven years, but it wasn't until October 26, 2025, when the Act 2 prayer line began discussing the subject, that I retrieved it. Now I have much more to add, as I have started preparing my presentation for the Acts 2 prayer line on the subject. There are some more revelations I have never seen or heard before, some were shared by my clients and friends with whom I discuss the topic. I am excited to share with you.

Politics is one of the most misunderstood subjects in almost all religions, and it is so by design. We often hear that Politics is horrible, horrific; that is not true. It is neutral, but humans have corrupted it. Furthermore, politics does not corrupt anyone; it just brings out the corruption that is already in you. It is one of the quickest and most powerful ways to expose your corruption. This subject has been further complicated by the author introducing two additional misconstrued subjects: Kingdom and Stewardship. Hence, this should be the most challenging of the books to write, yet it is not. To me, it is very straightforward. When you understand the Bible and why it was written, then all the subjects fall into place literally, because it is a political book. That is why Jesus said: *"But seek ye first the kingdom of God, and his righteousness; and all these things shall be added unto you"* (Matthew 6:33). He really means it. Your focus must be on His Kingdom, and He will reveal who you are, who others are, what you need to know, and what He has called you to do.

As you begin to read the Bible, you must understand that it is about the King, His Kingdom, His Subjects, and the restoration of that Kingdom. Thus, you will begin to comprehend that it is about politics, not in the context of Man's view, but God's, and thus at another level (Isaiah 55). Your eyes begin to be opened, and you start seeing what you have never seen before. Just like the disciples did, to the point they were willing to die for Jesus. You see, politics did not originate with man; it originated with God, it originated in Heaven. No, do not put down the book. Allow me to make my case. Yes, I know that politics has become so corrupt, crooked, shady, and selfish that we believe it is no longer associated with God. It is man that has corrupted it, just like he did religion, money, the earth, worship, and just about everything that God has given us.

There had to be a government in heaven; once there is more than one person, there must be rules, policies, and regulations for people to operate freely. Yes, even in a perfect environment. How do we know that? satan planned an opposition party against God, and in his campaigning, was able to win over one-third of the angels he politicized, and they were cast out with him. What form of government was in heaven? *"The Lord hath prepared his throne in the heavens; and his kingdom ruleth over all" (Psalm 103:19)*. It was a Kingdom form of government. Lucifer wanted to establish his form of government, and when he refused to do it God's way, he and his angels were cast out of heaven.

Jesus then brought this form of government to earth as was predicted. Jesus' first coming was a political one: *"For unto us a child is born, unto us a son is given: and the government shall be upon his shoulder: and his name shall be called Wonderful, Counsellor, The mighty God, The everlasting Father, The Prince of Peace. Of the increase of his government and peace there shall be no end, upon the throne of David, and upon his kingdom, to order it, and to establish it with judgment and with justice from henceforth even forever"* (Isaiah 9:6-7). He did not come to set up a new religion; Jesus came to establish a new government, a kingdom form of government. Daniel confirmed this: *"And in the days of these kings shall the God of heaven set up a kingdom, which shall never be destroyed: and the kingdom shall not be left to other people, but it shall break in pieces and consume all these kingdoms, and it shall stand forever"* (Daniel 2:44). Notice that Jesus did not bring another religion, instead He brought a kingdom form of government.

If you look deeper, politics is about health, jobs, infrastructure, tourism, laws, morals, mores, culture, governance, and religion—whatever human beings are involved in, there is, of necessity, a political aspect. How do you accomplish the aforementioned? How are they implemented? To benefit the greatest number of people. From a Kingdom perspective, how do you find a way to help those who are not among the majority? This is what God is about, and this is what politics should be about.

When we think of politics, we think of the personalities involved; we don't seek to understand what it is. We usually stop where man has taken us and don't really seek God's meaning. Let us delve into the Bible to see what it says about politics. As a faithful steward, you must allow the Spirit to reveal to you whether what I am saying is right or wrong.

CHAPTER 1

Why Do You Have Difficulty With Politics?

As an obedient steward of God, you are having difficulty because you don't know what God has to say about the subject. You have accepted what the world and the Church told you. It is okay, I did the same thing. Unfortunately, many churches discourage their members from getting involved politically. And the majority who do, ask them to vote, and that is the extent of their responsibility. However, this is being hypocritical; you are asking Jesus' disciples not to get involved politically, and then asking them to choose a non-disciple to rule over God's people. Do you understand how backward and ludicrous that is? Those who disobey and go further often have ulterior motives: they intend to benefit themselves, their church, or the leaders they have elected, who then help them with kickbacks.

To Whom Are You Listening?

The question you must answer is, have you read the Word of God to find out what God's position is on being involved in politics? I know that the subject totally turns off some of you. This is what the enemy wants so that you do not begin to experience the life God intended for you. Forget about what others have told you, including me; you cannot listen to anyone, not even your church, concerning any subject without you making sure that is what God is saying to you about it. And most importantly, what is He saying to you, personally? No one should be telling you what God wants you to be doing with your life; He will tell you Himself. Not that He will not put people in your sphere to help guide you and confirm what He has told you. Be very careful, you must know that it is God who sent them to speak to you. You must be aware that the enemy also sends people to you to advance his agenda. You must reach the place in your walk with the Lord where you can hear and know it is the voice of God. Jesus Himself says: *"My sheep hear my voice, and I know them, and they follow me"* (John 10:27). Because God is your Father, He is always speaking, just like you talk to your children if you love them and have their best interests at heart.

There are two ways you can hear the voice of God. First, you must be listening; there are so many voices and distractions clamoring for your attention. Thus, if you are not deliberately and intentionally listening, God's voice will be drowned out in the noise and confusion. Second, you must know His voice to know it is Him speaking. The only way this can be accomplished is that you must know Him personally, intimately, because you spend much time with Him in fellowship. If you don't, then you cannot follow. What is the best way to hear the voice of God? Spend time reading His Word, and as you do, listen because it is God speaking to you through His Word. Now, when you go about your day's activities, you will know His voice when He speaks. To get to know the voice of God, read the book in this series, "Kingdom Stewardship and ~~Relationship~~ Fellowship."

Your Thinking Must Change

Albert Einstein made a profound statement that applies here: "We can't solve problems by using the same thinking we used when we created them." We have serious issues with the politics that our current way of thinking has created. You must begin to think differently to solve them. God wants to help you. The Apostle Paul says: *"And be not conformed to this world: but be ye transformed by the renewing of your mind, that ye may prove what is that good, and acceptable, and perfect, will of God" (Romans 12:1)*. There must be a change in your thinking, it is your stinking thinking that has gotten you where you are now. When you change your thinking, you will discern what is good, acceptable to God, and His perfect will for your life. There can be no restrictions, limitations, or blinders. It is God you are dealing with, not man or his institutions. He wants to speak to you personally, read the book in this series, "Kingdom Stewardship and the Titles." One of the titles He gives you is that of a priest; therefore, you have access to God personally 24/7.

What Is Politics?

Politics is an integral part of our everyday life and will continue to be so in the future. Whether you want to or not, you will always be involved in politics. It is inescapable. Webster's Dictionary defines "Politics (noun) as the science (skill, art) of government; that part of ethics which has to do with the regulation and government of a nation or state, the preservation of its safety, peace, and prosperity, the defense of its existence and rights against foreign control or conquest, the augmentation of its strength and resources, and the protection of its citizens in their rights, with the preservation and improvement of their morals." It is very comprehensive. It covers all areas of your life and thus cannot be avoided. What could have been added to "the regulation and government of a nation or state" or a kingdom. The same principles apply.

If you strip it down to its core, politics is about governance, how we relate to each other personally, nationally, and internationally. It deals with the protection, rights, and morals of every citizen. You can see the influence of politics in your life daily in many different ways. The quality of the public schools or university your children attend, the health care you can access, and the way the police enforce laws and handle local crime are all directly affected by the political decisions made by lawmakers and government officials.

I was thinking long and hard about this concept of politics, and this is what the Spirit revealed to me: politics is about the people. Therefore, politicians should create policies that benefit the majority of the people. The policies are made with the best interests of the people in mind—not like it is now, where the policies are for a special group, for the political party in power, not for your family, or the majority of the people, whether they voted for you or not. What we have done is corrupt politics, making it about politicians, projects, prosperity, pride, payments, prejudice, profit, and popularity, rather than about people. We have taken it even to a lower level and made politics partisan with the two-party systems that we have around the world.

If politics is about people and policies, then it is part of our everyday life and impossible to escape. No matter how much you say, I don't want to be involved in politics. Even when we run from it, it runs after us and catches up. So, you need to stop saying I don't want to be political or get involved politically. Once you are alive, you are in politics; you are a political being; it is always and will always be about politics. It is the set of policies that help us live together in harmony and unity. Let us understand politics and use it for the greatest good of most people.

True humanity has corrupted politics and plotted ways to keep us ignorant. However, you do not have an excuse; there is readily available information, and the Word of God guides you into all truth (John 8:32).

So, what you must do is use the process that Jesus gave you for handling His emotions and griefs. First, you acknowledge that politics is a part of your life, whether you want it to or not. Second, accept and embrace politics; don't run from it. Yes, there will be some emotions associated with it—third, experience them. Don't try to suppress them; fourth, find those the Lord directs you to talk to about your experience. Fifth, you will regain the energy that was consumed by your emotions, which you can now use to invest in understanding this subject and exploring ways to change the dynamics around politics. The truth is, we cannot escape politics, no matter how hard we try; it permeates every aspect of our lives and society, so it's best not to try to hide from it. If you do, you will pay the consequences.

An Example

Let me show you how misunderstood this subject is. I had an interesting conversation with one of my cousins. She called and said she was disappointed in me because I was on the radio talking about politics instead of talking about God. I am a minister of the gospel. Yet she was talking to me about politics, but I cannot—and should not—be discussing it. Here is what she added: They told their ministers to stay out of politics. Hence, some churches muzzle their ministers from discussing politics; even if God wants them to speak out, they cannot because the churches are paying their salaries, so the church members decide what they can speak about. This is one of the reasons why I am an independent pastor. Now I understand why some ministers are unable to participate in the radio broadcast. Not because I know that does not make it right, I will show you that part of your responsibility is to speak out about the wrongs the government is doing.

My cousin wants to tell me how to live my life and then dictate what I can and cannot do; it doesn't matter if God is the one who told me to speak. That is the problem; it is about control, not about the policies that can benefit most of the people. Just accept that my party is in power and whatever they do is right, accept it as gospel.

What is Politics About?

Politics is about people, and the emphasis is on service, serving the people of your jurisdiction. We fail to realize that the Government has the greatest influence and control. Why would God then leave it up to anyone and not intervene? The government, that is, politicians, have the power to legislate, and they do, based on their belief system or the philosophy by which they live. Laws create the values of society, which produce the moral standards; the issue is not whether they are right or wrong. They are responsible for the country's moral climate. When these are combined, they produce the culture of society. Culture is the lifestyle of a people; our values are a consequence of our moral standing, which is because of our laws, which come from leadership, the legislator's philosophy or belief system.

That is why everybody wants to get into government. Why? They want their belief system or philosophy to become law, thereby creating values and moral standards for their country. This creates the kind of culture they want. For example, that's why gays run for political offices, they understand that here is where power lies, they can create laws that are congruent with their lifestyle, in other words, they want to make their culture. This is the reality. We are not the only ones; all human beings' objective is to be fruitful, multiply, fill, subdue, and have dominion over the earth with whatever they are given, including their belief system. Even Nations do this when they invade other countries, for the same reason, they want to impose their belief system on them. Understanding this, Jesus restored the government He created in Genesis. So, you must get involved.

When It Is Not About People

Here is what happens: when it is not about people, most Politicians get rid of most people who voted for them and only deal with those who are part of their party system. They create policies that favor individuals within their party system, often ignoring those who helped them get elected. What are the results? Our objectives and motives become selfish and self-centered, as Judge Mitchell so eloquently puts it. It will be about the party system, not the country, and definitely not about the people, except for whom they choose to support.

This does not take place in a vacuum; politics is an integral part of our daily lives. Hence, it is based on decision-making and who you choose to rule your life. It will bring life or death as the Apostle Paul points out: *"Know ye not, that to whom ye yield yourselves servants to obey, his servants ye are to whom ye obey; whether of sin unto death, or of obedience unto righteousness? But God be thanked, that ye were the servants of sin, but ye have obeyed from the heart that form of doctrine which was delivered to you. Being then made free from sin, ye became the servants of righteousness (Romans 6:16-18).*

I believe our world is in the mess we are in because God's people, many who call ourselves Christians, are not living out their faith daily, and we are not obedient stewards in all areas of our lives, including politics. It cannot be a separate entity in life. You are a holistic person; your life is not segmented, disconnected, or disjointed; it is one. When you try to separate it into segments, it creates a great deal of dissonance, which leads to unbearable stress. You become discouraged, disheartened, depressed, and eventually hopeless.

CHAPTER 2

The Kingdom And Politics

The Kingdom of God is about politics. They cannot be separated.

Heaven's Opposition Party

Satan was the first one to misuse and abuse God's political system. *"How art thou fallen from heaven, O Lucifer, son of the morning! How art thou cut down to the ground, which didst weaken the nations! For thou hast said in thine heart, I will ascend into heaven, I will exalt my throne above the stars of God: I will sit also upon the mount of the congregation, in the sides of the north: I will ascend above the heights of the clouds; I will be like the most High. Yet thou shalt be brought down to hell, to the sides of the pit"* (Isaiah 14:12-15). He was and is in opposition to God's form of government. In his campaign on earth, satan got Adam and Eve to join his opposition party. *"When the woman saw that the tree was good for food, and that it was pleasant to the eyes, and a tree to be desired to make one wise, she took of the fruit thereof, and did eat, and gave also unto her husband with her; and he did eat. And the eyes of them both were opened, and they knew that they were naked; and they sewed fig leaves together, and made themselves aprons. And they heard the voice of the Lord God walking in the garden in the cool of the day: and*

Adam and his wife hid themselves from the presence of the Lord God amongst the trees of the garden. And the Lord God called unto Adam, and said unto him, Where art thou? And he said, I heard thy voice in the garden, and I was afraid, because I was naked; and I hid myself. And he said, Who told thee that thou wast naked? Hast thou eaten of the tree, whereof I commanded thee that thou shouldest not eat?" (Genesis 3:6-11). Thus, Adam and Eve struggled with God's system of government and went against it, and we have been struggling with this concept of politics ever since. The enemy is having a field day, confusing you and getting you to follow his form of government and not God's.

Who Is The Bible About

Here are the instructions that Jesus has given to us as His children: *"Search the Scriptures; for in them ye think ye have eternal life: and they are they which testify of me"* (John 5:39). Jesus is here saying you must understand the Word of God; if not, you will misinterpret it and continue to make false interpretations and thus ruin your life and the lives of others by making wrong decisions. Notice that He is saying Scriptures are not about a what, but have always been about a who. Who is the Bible about? It is about the King, His Kingdom, His subjects, and His desire to extend His Kingdom to earth, which He did. Adam and Eve gave it to the enemy (Matthew 12:26-28). Jesus came to restore what He originally intended.

What Government Did Jesus Establish

Jesus came and took it back, and when He did, He restored His form of government, His original political system. Hence, Jesus' first coming was a political one. How can we come to that conclusion: *"For unto us a child is born, unto us a son is given: and the government shall be upon his shoulder: and his name shall be called*

Wonderful, Counsellor, The mighty God, The everlasting Father, The Prince of Peace. Of the increase of his government and peace, there shall be no end, upon the throne of David, and upon his kingdom, to order it, and to establish it with judgment and with justice from henceforth even forever. The zeal of the Lord of hosts will perform this" (Isaiah 9:6-7). It was a Kingdom form of government, which was political. How do we know? He tells us it was going to be on the throne of David and His Kingdom. Is there any more confirmation that it was a Kingdom form of government? The Prophet Daniel tells us: *"And in the days of these kings shall the God of heaven set up a kingdom, which shall never be destroyed: and the kingdom shall not be left to other people, but it shall break in pieces and consume all these kingdoms, and it shall stand forever" (Daniel 2:44).* As was predicted by the prophet Isaiah, Jesus came during the reign of the Roman kingdom. When Jesus came, He restored His Kingdom; it is indeed spiritual now; however, it becomes physical through our lifestyle. We reveal the Kingdom by living out the beatitudes and the rest of the Word as Kingdom citizens.

Jesus came and restored God's Kingdom form of Government, which He created when He created this universe. How do we know it was a Kingdom He created for Adam, Eve, and for us? Jesus Himself told us: *"Then shall the King say unto them on his right hand, Come, ye blessed of my Father, inherit the kingdom prepared for you from the foundation of the world" (Matthew 25:34).* Since God is the same yesterday, today, and forever (Hebrews 13:8) and does not change (Malachi 3:6), He restored the Kingdom He originally created. We can agree that the government will be the same on earth as it is in Heaven for several reasons. The primary reason is that we are made in His image (Genesis 1:26-28, 5:1-3), so He will give us what He has. The second is: *"The Lord hath prepared his throne in the heavens; and his kingdom ruleth over all" (Psalm 103:19).* Third, it is a part of the prayer He taught us, His disciples, to pray: *"Thy kingdom come, Thy will be done in earth, as it is in heaven." (Matthew 6:10).*

God's Manifesto and Constitution

Once sin entered our world, what do all forms of governments—Kingdom, Dictatorship, or Democracy—use to tell their citizens how they should live and what is expected of them? They use a manifesto, which tells you what they are going to do, and a constitution to tell you how to live as a citizen. Before sin, there was no need for a manifesto or a constitution because God would come down regularly and communicate with Adam and Eve (Genesis 3:8). After sin is eradicated, there will be no need for them, because Jesus will live among us (Revelation 21:1-4). Well, man got this concept from God. Some manifestos and constitutions are written or passed down through generations. Here is what Article 2 Timothy, section 3, subsection 16-17 of His constitution tells us what His constitution is for: *"All scripture is given by inspiration of God, and is profitable for doctrine, for reproof, for correction, for instruction in righteousness: That the man of God may be perfect, thoroughly furnished unto all good works" (2 Timothy 3:16-17).* What does doctrine mean: A doctrine is a rule or principle that forms the basis of a belief, theory, or policy, a body of ideas, particularly in religion, taught to people as truthful or correct' (Encarta Dictionary). 'A particular principle, position, or policy is taught or advocated by a religion or government' (Dictionary.com). The Scriptures are God's manifesto and constitution to us, His creatures. Every kingdom and government has them. God's Kingdom had a manifesto and constitution before any earthly King or Government. The Bible is God's constitution regarding how He wants His people, disciples, to live in His Kingdom. It explains who our King is and what He expects, as well as who you are, your rights, responsibilities, freedom, and benefits. People will tell you what they are if you don't know what they are. Most will not tell you for your benefit, but for their own. That is precisely what politicians are doing today, where are God's people to stand up and speak out against this atrocity?

Without understanding God's constitution, you will always live below your potential. You can never truly experience freedom without others trying to take away your benefits and rights. Man came along and corrupted what God had instituted, just as He had given everything else; we have twisted it so that we can get what we want out of it. That is why, as God's people, we should be involved in the political system to implement His form of government.

The Kingdom Was Always God's Plan

We already established that when He created this universe, it was a Kingdom (Matthew 25:34). Let me show you that this plan continues throughout the Bible and never stops. We can agree that in the Bible, the terms 'nation' and 'kingdom' are often used synonymously. Here is what God said to Abraham when He called Him: *"Now the Lord had said unto Abram, Get thee out of thy country, and from thy kindred, and from thy father's house, unto a land that I will shew thee: And I will make of thee a great nation, and I will bless thee, and make thy name great; and thou shalt be a blessing: And I will bless them that bless thee, and curse him that curseth thee: and in thee shall all families of the earth be blessed"* *(Genesis 12:1-3).* God's objective was to make Abraham into a great nation. This nation was not limited to one group of people, nor was it just his descendants. He was going to make a difference to all families of the earth. This is the kingdom God was hoping that this great nation would have established. How can I say it is a kingdom?

Listen to what God told Abraham and Sarah: *"Neither shall thy name any more be called Abram, but thy name shall be Abraham; for a father of many nations have I made thee. And I will make thee exceeding fruitful, and I will make nations of thee, and kings shall come out of thee. And I will establish my covenant between me and thee and thy seed after thee in their generations for an everlasting covenant, to be a God unto thee, and to thy seed after thee. And I will give unto thee, and to thy seed after thee, the land wherein thou art a stranger, all the land of Canaan, for an everlasting possession; and I will be their God"* (Genesis 17:5-8). Very often, we forget Sarah out of the equation; God did not. This is what He says of Sarah: *"And God said unto Abraham, As for Sarai thy wife, thou shalt not call her name Sarai, but Sarah shall her name be. And I will bless her, and give thee a son also of her: yea, I will bless her, and she shall be a mother of nations; kings of people shall be of her"* (Genesis 17:15-16). When we discuss Abraham, we often overlook Sarah, who was an integral part of everything they did. That is one of the reasons why I believe He was so successful. Take note that kings emerged from both. Now only kings can produce kings. Let us see what the Bible says in Genesis 1:11-12: *"And God said, Let the earth bring forth grass, the herb yielding seed, and the fruit tree yielding fruit after his kind, whose seed is in itself, upon the earth: and it was so. And the earth brought forth grass, and herb yielding seed after his kind, and the tree yielding fruit, whose seed was in itself, after his kind: and God saw that it was good"* (See also Genesis 1:21, 24-25). The Bible establishes the principle that kind can only produce kind. This is repeated 10 times in these verses, which means perfection, completeness, the correct number of times. Only what is, can produce after its kind. So, dogs can only produce dogs; it does not matter how many kinds they are. Humans can only produce humans; kings can only produce kings.

Kingdom and Nation

When He called Israel into existence, Israel was a nation, a nation is run by government, policies, and politics, with God as their King. Just like He did with Adam and Eve, who were also kings. So are we *(Revelations 1:5-6, 5:9-10, 1 Peter 2:9)*. In Exodus 18, Jethro helped Moses set up the judicial system that is used by many nations of the world today—the establishment of the judicial system is a part of the government's responsibilities. Then God used Moses, Israel's political leader, to help institute the health laws, which you can read about in the book of Leviticus. This is another responsibility of the government. God established prophets and priests to help the nation, or the Kingdom of Israel. So, everyone was involved politically. That is the way it is in God's system of government: there is no separation, segregation, or isolation. The enemy comes along and creates separation and division; thus, it is manufactured. Then they asked for a king, which disrupted God's system of government, and they suffered the consequences (1 Kings 8). Thus, the nation that God created was a Kingdom.

Nation and Kingdom are still God's plan: Here is what the Apostle Peter tells us: *"But ye are a chosen generation, a royal priesthood, an holy nation, a peculiar people; that ye should shew forth the praises of him who hath called you out of darkness into his marvellous light"* **(1 Peter 2:9)**. Here we see the concept of a nation which is synonymous with a kingdom. Just in case you do not believe, note we are a royal priesthood, that is to say, priests who are kings.

Have You Embraced the Kingdom?

I believe the main reason why many get into trouble in politics is that they have not yet learned to embrace the Kingdom. If you understand and operate within the context of God's Kingdom, many of your problems, including political ones, will be solved. This is what Jesus said: *"But seek ye first the kingdom of God, and his righteousness; and all these things shall be added unto you. Take therefore no thought for the morrow: for the morrow shall take thought for the things of itself. Sufficient unto the day is the evil thereof"* (Matthew 6:33-34). If you seek to know God and His Kingdom, then you will be better equipped to handle the conflicts, struggles, and disappointments you encounter. Because, in a kingdom, the King is responsible for his citizens. His success is determined by how well his subjects are doing.

How Many Kingdoms Are There?

There are two kingdoms that exist, and you are constantly being ruled by one. There is no in between; you don't have a kingdom, even though you behave like you do sometimes. The controversy today centers on kingdoms, thereby involving politics. God has His Kingdom: *"The Lord hath prepared his throne in the heavens; and his kingdom ruleth over all"* (Psalm 103:19). satan has his: *"And if Satan cast out Satan, he is divided against himself; how shall then his kingdom stand?"* (Matthew 12:26). The one he stole from Adam and Eve, because he cannot create one.

Even in the Old Testament, the fight was over these same two kingdoms. They were always fighting to see whose god (King) was the most powerful. Israel's biggest political mistake was when they chose a king because they wanted to be like the other nations. Remember God told them: *"I will be thy king: where is any other that may save thee in all thy cities? And thy judges of whom thou saidst, Give me a king and princes? (Hosea 13:10).* God wanted to be Israel's King and rule over them. Instead, this is what they wanted: *"And said unto him, Behold, thou art old, and thy sons walk not in thy ways: now make us a king to judge us like all the nations. But the thing displeased Samuel when they said, Give us a king to*

*judge us. And Samuel prayed unto the Lord. And the Lord said...,
Hearken unto the voice of the people in all that they say unto thee: for
they have not rejected thee, but they have rejected me, that I should not
reign over them"* (1 Samuel 8:5-7). They no longer wanted God as
their King. They wanted to be like the other nations. You make
the same mistake. God wants to be your king and rule your life,
but you want to be like others, wanting what they have, doing
what they do, when He wants you to be different *(Romans 12:1)*.

The Kingdoms of this World

He warned them about the consequences of trying to be like
the other nations. Here is a perfect example of what the kingdom
of the enemy is about. You must remember that satan does not
have a kingdom any longer. God warned the children of Israel not
to choose a king but to allow Him to be their King. He gave them
the reasons why not; you can read them in *1 Kings 8:11-19*. Yet,
they insisted they wanted a king. Whenever you go against God's
politics, your loss will always be substantial. You are asking how
can I say God's politics? You will agree that a Kingdom is a form of
government. Government is about politics and policies. I agree;
His policies are different, as the King of kings and Lord of lords,
He operates differently. That is why you have difficulty with His
politics. Here is why: *"Seek ye the Lord while he may be found, call
ye upon him while he is near: Let the wicked forsake his way, and the
unrighteous man his thoughts: and let him return unto the Lord, and
he will have mercy upon him; and to our God, for he will abundantly
pardon. For my thoughts are not your thoughts, neither are your ways
my ways, saith the Lord. For as the heavens are higher than the earth,
so are my ways higher than your ways, and my thoughts than your
thoughts. For as the rain cometh down, and the snow from heaven,
and returneth not thither, but watereth the earth, and maketh it bring
forth and bud, that it may give seed to the sower, and bread to the*

eater: So shall my word be that goeth forth out of my mouth: it shall not return unto me void, but it shall accomplish that which I please, and it shall prosper in the thing whereto I sent it" (Isaiah 55:6-11). The Kingdom suggests that you are not in charge; the King is. You are owned by, and thus you are working for the King. You are not your own, and in God's Kingdom, not only were you made by Him, but He redeemed you. So, you are His twice.

CHAPTER 3

A Biblical View of Politics

When you think of politics, who comes to mind? Politicians. These are seen as the government, which is false. In a democracy, we all make up the government; the politicians are our representatives. Man did not institute the concept of Government; it originated with God. Hence, there is nothing wrong with politics. It is a part of life, thus you need to embrace it. God is not anti-government; there is a government in Heaven, you heard me right. Government is for governance, once people are present there must of necessity be governed under all circumstances, a perfect or imperfect environment *"In those days there was no king in Israel: every man did that which was right in his own eyes." (Judges 17:6)*. The exact words are repeated in *Judges 21:25*. The Lord established laws, rules and regulations, here are some of them *Genesis 1:26-28,* He told them to be fruitful, multiply, replenish, subdue, have dominion. In Genesis 2:15, He talks to them about taking care of the garden. Here is what God says in Genesis 2:16-17: *"And the Lord God commanded the man, saying, Of every tree of the garden thou mayest freely eat: But of the tree of the knowledge of good and evil, thou shalt not eat of it: for in the day that thou eatest thereof thou shalt surely die."* Whenever and wherever governance exists, there is a necessity for politics.

Jesus and Government

Do you know that the first mention of government in the Bible is associated with Jesus? Thus, it is political: *"For unto us a child is born, unto us a son is given: and the government shall be upon his shoulder: and his name shall be called Wonderful, Counsellor, The mighty God, The everlasting Father, The Prince of Peace. Of the increase of his government and peace there shall be no end, upon the throne of David, and upon his kingdom, to order it, and to establish it with judgment and with justice from henceforth even forever"* (Isaiah 9:6-7). According to Isaiah, Jesus came to set up His Kingdom form of government. This is a rare Hebrew word which means "the burden of authority" "Kingship or Scepter." He did not come to establish another religion; that is what most of us expected. Instead, He came to establish His form of governance, similar to the one in heaven.

The Kingdom

When you go back to Genesis, God created the heaven and earth *(Genesis 1:1)*, this was a Kingdom He established for his subjects and gave them authority, power to rule, and to dominate: *"And God said, Let us make man in our image, after our likeness: and let them have dominion over the fish of the sea, and over the fowl of the air, and over the cattle, and over all the earth, and over every creeping thing that creepeth upon the earth. So, God created man in his own image, in the image of God created he him; male and female created he them. And God blessed them, and God said unto them, Be fruitful, and multiply, and replenish the earth, and subdue it: and have dominion over the fish of the sea, and over the fowl of the air, and over every living thing that moveth upon the earth"* (Genesis 1:26-28). Once man sinned, Jesus, the last Adam, came to restore the Kingdom that was stolen. God thus rules and overrules in the affairs of man. God has the final say in what happens in His Kingdom—sets up and takes down kings, which is a political process.

Praying For Politicians

Here is further evidence that God is not opposed to politics. He asked us to pray for the politicians: *"I exhort therefore, that, first of all, supplications, prayers, intercessions, and giving of thanks, be made for all men; For kings, and for all that are in authority; that we may lead a quiet and peaceable life in all godliness and honesty. For this is good and acceptable in the sight of God our Saviour"* (1 Timothy 2:1-3). This is God's will. This means it is your responsibility to work along with your elected representatives. In like manner, if God's disciples are elected, you can pray for them as well.

God Gave the Gift of Government

Here was another eye opener for me, one of the gifts that God has given to His children is in the area governing: *"And God hath set some in the church, first apostles, secondarily prophets, thirdly teachers, after that miracles, then gifts of healings, helps, governments, diversities of tongues"* (1 Corinthians 12:28). These are church members. God always has His people involved in politics because it originated with Him. What does this mean? Based on this false teaching, there are those whom the Lord gifted in government who missed their calling because they did not understand that the Lord had gifted them in this field. Many do not know that the Lord is the one who should called them to their vocation: *"I therefore, the prisoner of the Lord, beseech you that ye walk worthy of the vocation wherewith ye are called, With all lowliness and meekness, with longsuffering, forbearing one another in love; Endeavoring to keep the unity of the Spirit in the bond of peace"* (Ephesians 4:1-3). He goes even further; He tells you how to behave on the job—don't exalt yourself, exercise patience. Whatever you do, make sure it is done in love. Do not leave your faith behind; promote an atmosphere of peace and harmony. Then like Joseph your business or whoever you work for will prosper: *"And it came to pass from the time that he had made him overseer in his house, and over all that he had, that the Lord blessed the Egyptian's house for Joseph's sake; and the blessing of the Lord was upon all that he had in the house, and in the field"* (Genesis 39:5). Your presence will cause others to be blessed, even as politicians.

God is Always Involved in the Political Process

The Lord does not leave anything up to chance: *"Until thou know that the most High ruleth in the kingdom of men, and giveth it to whomsoever he will"* (Daniel 4:32). Daniel continues to make this point and was qualified to do so; he served under four different Kings and three different Kingdoms. This is usually unheard of in the political arena. The New King or Politician typically brings in who they want, and often it is their friends and family members.

Daniel knew and acknowledged he was place there by God: *"This matter is by the decree of the watchers, and the demand by the word of the holy ones: to the intent that the living may know that the most High ruleth in the kingdom of men, and giveth it to whomsoever he will, and setteth up over it the basest of men"* (Daniel 4:17). That is because this is the area that God called Daniel to accomplish. Why? This is one of the areas in which he was gifted, and God calls us according to our gifts. You might have more questions than answers; however, you must remember that He does not think like us. Like a parent, He sees what our children do not see. You must learn to trust Him.

Why You Must Be Involved?

In the physical realm, Government is a greater force than religion right now. Why, because they make the laws, create the values or morals for any country, not the church. The government is critical to you. Everyone wants and is preoccupied with it. Government is so important that you want to be in it, or you are thinking or talking about it. Look at how influential they are; your government determines what kind of lifestyle you will live, what foods you have access to, what clothes you can buy, and what vehicles you can drive. Don't fool yourself; you are not in heaven yet. That is why you don't just want any government, but a specific one—one that is kind, compassionate, and full of understanding. That is the one Jesus brought for us to be a part of His government.

Politicians are Ministers of God

I was trying to figure out why, in the English form of government, politicians are referred to as ministers. Then I read Romans 13, and I discovered that it is about politics God's way. Here is God's instructions to His Kingdom citizens, stewards, and disciples through the Apostle Paul: *"Let every soul be subject unto the higher powers. For there is no power but of God: the powers that be are ordained of God....For he is the minister of God to thee for good. But if thou do that which is evil, be afraid; for he beareth not the sword in vain: for he is the minister of God, a revenger to execute wrath upon him that doeth evil" (Romans 13:1,4).* Higher powers here refer to those in authority—the civil leaders. God is telling you through His steward, the Apostle Paul, that you must be subject to them. Here is the reason why God can instruct you to do this, there is no power on the face of the earth that is more powerful than Him. You get your power from Me. Since this is true, how can you separate Church and State when the rulers are ministers of God?

The Bible then goes on to say, these are the ministers of God. This is mentioned on two occasions. Their responsibility is to protect God's people from evil. After all, they are God's representatives, His ministers. That is why, in the English system, they are referred to as ministers with different portfolios. Thus, you have the Minister of Tourism, the Minister of Finance, the Minister of Infrastructure, and so on.

Why Does God Want You To Be Subject to Them?

He gives you the answer through His prophet Daniel: *"Daniel answered and said, Blessed be the name of God forever and ever: for wisdom and might are his: And he changeth the times and the seasons: he removeth kings, and setteth up kings: he giveth wisdom unto the wise, and knowledge to them that know understanding: He revealeth the deep and secret things: he knoweth what is in the darkness, and the light dwelleth with him"* (Daniel 2:20-22). God is in control; He created everything and is involved in its day-to-day operations. He did not just create and leave us on our own. I know for some of you that sounds impossible, especially when you see what is taking place today in the political arena. God does not have to prove Himself to anyone that He is God. You either accept or reject Him. That is what many choose to do, and thus our world is going to hell in a handbasket.

God is all-knowing, always present, and all-wise; thus, He changes the times and seasons, setting up kings and taking them down. He wants to impart knowledge, understanding, and wisdom to you, so that you can discern His will for you and be able to help those around you. Thus, as His steward, be a part of His overall politics of advancing the Kingdom of God.

When You Resist Them, You Are Resisting God

When you oppose those whom God chooses to be in politics, you are resisting Him, says the wise man Paul: *"Whosoever therefore resisteth the power, resisteth the ordinance of God: and they that resist shall receive to themselves damnation" (Romans 13:2).* You will suffer the consequences, only if they are doing the will of God. If they are doing their own thing, then they will have to deal with the Lord and whatever He chooses to do with them. Not because it is the Lord who placed you there means you can do as you please. There are several purposes why He has chosen you. You need to discover what they are and, by His grace, strive to fulfill them.

What is the Purpose of Government?

As you read earlier, God establishes kings and governments for His Glory. They have their roles and responsibilities to play in the lives of His people. The Apostle continues: *"For rulers are not a terror to good works, but to the evil. Wilt thou then not be afraid of the power? Do that which is good, and thou shalt have praise of the same" (Romans 13:3).* Their primary responsibility is to do what is right and pleasing in God's sight, not what they want. What are some of the government's purposes?

To Restrain Evil

Government is not here to make you good—only God can do that. They can't legislate morality, but every law that is passed affects our morals, values, mores, and culture. And so, it is true that no law can be legislated to make you love me. That is why there must be a law to make sure that you do not kill me. True, you can't legislate morality; however, you must legislate against immorality. No law on earth can make you honest; thus, there must be a law to keep you from stealing. No law can stop you from lying; there must be a law to keep you from committing perjury.

Help The Poor

One of the Government's responsibilities is to help the poor. This is what the Lord said to King Nebuchadnezzar: *"Wherefore, O king, let my counsel be acceptable unto thee, and break off thy sins by righteousness, and thine iniquities by shewing mercy to the poor; if it may be a lengthening of thy tranquility" (Daniel 4:27)*. The greatest evil they must protect, is the oppression and abuse of the poor.

Administer Justice

"Of the increase of his government and peace there shall be no end, upon the throne of David, and upon his kingdom, to order it, and to establish it with judgment and with justice from henceforth even forever. The zeal of the Lord of hosts will perform this" (Isaiah 9:7). Even today, the government is responsible for the administration of Justice. With God's government, He will make sure that justice is served judiciously. This is what the prophet Micah told the nation of Israel: *"He has shown you, O mortal, what is good. And what does the Lord require of you? To act justly and to love mercy and to walk humbly with your God" (Micah 6:8)*. This is a requirement for all human beings. This is also a political statement. The government administers justice, and politicians appoint judges to the bench. Furthermore, the Lord expects the political leaders to show mercy. *"And whereas they commanded to leave the stump of the tree roots; thy kingdom shall be sure unto thee, after that thou shalt have known that the heavens do rule. Wherefore, O king, let my counsel be acceptable unto thee, and break off thy sins by righteousness, and thine iniquities by shewing mercy to the poor; if it may be a lengthening of thy tranquillity" (Daniel 4:26-27)*. Showing mercy to the poor is another form of justice. We are involved in Politics whether we want to or not; it is impossible to escape. In God's economy, He always made provision for the poor.

A Personal Experience

I was speaking with a young, aspiring politician, Sis. Rogers, who is a member of the denomination to which I belong. We were talking, and I wanted to know what her plans were for the future. She said she wanted to be a politician. I was excited. First of all, many young people are unsure of what God's calling is in their lives. Second, was the freshness of this young lady, who declared her desire to be involved in the political process. The Spirit had begun revealing to me that the way the Church was teaching about this concept was not Biblical. Thus, her response was refreshing and encouraging.

Furthermore, it was during our conversation that the Spirit revealed to me the reason why politics is so prevalent in the church. Most church members are told not to get involved in politics. As you have learned, this is impossible because we are political beings; we must now use that energy in church politics. Hence, if you do not get involved in the politics of your community and country, then you must get involved in church, workplace, or family politics because it is impossible to remain uninvolved in politics. It is a part of God's plan for man. God hardwired us for the political process.

That is why it is considered such a bad thing when it is introduced in Church, for more than one reason. The Church is perceived as hypocritical; it teaches that you should not be involved in politics, just vote, and you have done your duty. Yet, politics is so flagrant in the Church, people are turned off because the Church is living a double standard. There is nothing wrong with politics in the church; it is just that we have corrupted it, just like we do in our government. Once there is more than one person, there is a need for governance. There must be rules, regulations, boundaries, mores, morals; where does your freedom end and mine begin?

Due to the double standard and hypocrisy, it is perceived as nastier and more wicked than it actually is in the world. The reason I believe is that it is not expected in the Church. This turns many people off, and some leave the church or seek another group to worship.

Herd Mentality

One of Christianity's biggest problems is the tendency toward a herd mentality. We refuse to think for ourselves because we struggle with thinking, and this struggle has been exacerbated by not being rewarded for our thoughts. But, the opposite is true in the business world: the more you think and the more you do outside the box, the greater the reward. Businesses want to be different even if they are selling the same products or providing the same services.

God is very heavy into differences and rewards those who are different in Him. In Church, we are often afraid of differences, to the extent that we isolate ourselves to remain distinct. Businesses do the opposite; they expose themselves because they are different. There are those religions that are so different that they hide and produce their own communities, campgrounds, and schools. They have developed the Fort Mentality, where there are planned times when they open the gates, interact with the community, and let in some who want to come in and join us. The difference is that in business, the differences are designed to be exposed to the public, not to be hidden from it, as religions often do.

CHAPTER 4

Confusion Over Church and Politics

There is a great deal of confusion surrounding politics, and sadly, many religions that offer guidance have contributed to this confusion and frustration. For example, we discourage believers from running for politics, even if the Lord called them to this vocation (Ephesians 4:1-3), and then ask them to vote for those the Lord did not call to run. That is a big contradiction, because we are asking them to vote for non-believers and then complain about what an atrocious job our politicians are doing. What do you expect if they are not disciples of Jesus?

The Church and Politics

I remembered when my denomination used to discourage its members from becoming Lawyers, because, as was taught, all lawyers are liars. Now that the Church has a great need for lawyers, I suppose that means we want them to lie on our behalf now. No Church can continue to exist without having lawyers on its staff or easy access to them. Similarly, many denominations have discouraged their members from getting involved in the political arena. The main reason is that all politicians are corrupt.

I declare to you that this is one of the reasons our world is in the mess it is in politically. We do not understand politics from God's perspective, because we have made it a taboo subject. Let me illustrate what I mean with an incident that I encountered.

Some Leadership's View

I was discussing the issue with two conference presidents of our denomination and making the point vehemently, as I usually do, "As God's people, we need to get involved in the political process." While making my case, they were throwing cold water on what I was saying. They thought what I was saying was foolish, ridiculous, and ludicrous. They responded by telling me that it's not possible for Christians because politics is too corrupt, nasty, and defiled; thus, God's people should not get involved in that process; it will eat them alive. Slowly, I began to back off, as I was not making any progress; however, we continued our conversation.

One of the gentlemen began to relate a story of being recruited by the Masons. The main reason was that they admired the way he persuaded people to join the church through his evangelistic preaching series. They wanted him to join them because they saw the benefits they would derive from having him as part of their organization. He would be a great asset to their organization. They were very persistent; they met with him on several occasions and wrote him a letter, and as he read it, the words began to glow on the page. To make sure he was not suffering from an optical illusion, he skipped to the bottom of the page to see if this was real. Wherever he read, it began to glow. He said there were three things they were offering him: you can have all the money, fame, and women you want. He said, 'I have one wife, and even she is too much for me; what will I do with more?' He was very adamant, dug his heels in, and said no, no, no. I don't want to be a part of your organization.

When he was through, I chimed in, how is that different from getting involved in politics? Here was what you believed was an evil, corrupt, nasty organization that was trying to recruit and use you, and you said no. Just as you stood up to them, if God calls anyone into politics, He will give them the same power to resist the evil in politics as well. I continued, if God has called them, they should answer the call to become involved in politics. They should not listen to what others are saying, especially if they are being encouraged to go against God's wishes. I reminded them that we are constantly being recruited by the enemy of souls daily. The same way you are living now is the same way you will be living if you get into politics. It is not politics that corrupted you; you were corrupt before you entered politics. It is being manifested, unfortunately, on a larger scale. It was their time to be quiet and really listen. They did not say anything; I believe the Lord showed them another way to look at it. There was little pushback this time; however, they did not concede that it is okay for God's people to be involved in politics.

Here is the reason I believe it is so difficult to accept what the Bible says about politics. The indoctrination of believers not having any involvement in this process is so intense that it is difficult to admit we are wrong on this subject. This becomes even more challenging if your church teaches that it has the truth. Then it means that if we have to change our minds, we no longer possess the truth, and instead of correcting the wrong, we suffer, and those whom we lead also suffer, because they are the ones we can help. After all, God gave them the gift of government. The entire community suffers because they are missing out on what God has in store for them through this person or persons.

There are times when we say things we haven't fully thought through; we only say them because we've heard others repeat them. First, they sound true. Second, the more they are repeated, the more we begin to believe they are the truth. If you keep repeating a lie long enough, you will eventually start to believe it is true. To know the truth, you must consult who is truth, the Father, Son, Holy Spirit, and the Word.

You Will Not Hear God's Call

With this kind of teaching, it means that if God is calling you to political office, you will not hear his voice, since you have been told that you should not be involved in this field. I am convinced that many whom God called to politics have missed that calling because of how the church has taught this subject. Here is the reality: it is impossible to avoid being involved in the political process. You are involved whether you want to be or not. Politics encompasses a wide range of issues, including health, jobs, infrastructure, tourism, laws, morals, mores, culture, governance, religion, and more. Wherever there are human beings, there is a necessity for politics. All these affect your life daily. How do you accomplish the aforementioned? How are they done to benefit the greatest number of people? Then how do you find a way to help those who are not a part of the majority? This is what politics is about. Not because they are in the minority, you ignore them, their needs also need to be met. This is a criterion that indicates you are called to be a politician; you possess the gift of governance. You are not just in it to get, but to give and look out for the least of these.

When you think of politics, you usually think of the personalities involved in it; you don't seek to understand what it is. You normally stop where man has taken it and don't really seek its real meaning. Should you be involved in politics is a question that many believe we should not ask God, and therefore do not ask, because it is considered corrupt and God is thought to have nothing to do with it. However, this is not true, and He will reveal to you in His Word what this topic is all about. Let us continue exploring what the Bible has to say about it. You must allow the Spirit to reveal to you whether what I have written is true or false.

Who Should You Be Seeking?

Jesus Himself says, you shall know the truth and the truth shall set you free (John 8:32). Your problem stems from a lack of understanding truth; you were taught and have limited truth to a body of doctrines, which is what your church teaches. Thus, you hear, we have the truth, no, you don't, because if you have the truth, then you have the way and you have the life (John 14:6). How come you don't hear any church claiming they are the way and the life? Likewise, you cannot claim to have the truth. The truth is not words, doctrines, or sayings; it is much more than that. Truth is a person, hence Jesus is Truth (John 14:6), The Word is Truth (John 17:17), because it is about Jesus (John 1:1, 14), God is Truth (Deuteronomy 32:4), the Spirit is Truth (John 16:13). Thus, the Truth you need to know is God, who is a person, not your church's doctrines. He will reveal to you how to live out the doctrines. So, Truth must possess you, not you possess truth, because you cannot. It did not originate in this realm, so it is above our pay grade. Truth is pure; it cannot be corrupted, manipulated, maligned, misinterpreted, or misconstrued; that is how pure it is. It destroys lies in its paths. How do you access truth? By accepting Jesus as your Lord and Savior, so that He can possess you and reveal Himself to you in all areas of your life. This is one of the reasons for this series of books. To know how to accomplish this, turn to the back of the book. You will become one of His stewards and disciples and allow truth to possess you.

Without a knowledge of Truth, which is not your religion, people will continue to keep you in bondage and have you like a puppet on a string. The way of the Kingdom of Man, which is actually satan' kingdom, does everything in its power to control everyone. They accomplish this by keeping or withholding pertinent information about your history that you should be aware of.

No One to Blame, But Yourself

You cannot blame others for your ignorance on any subject. Here is what the Bible says: *"Study to shew thyself approved unto God, a workman that needeth not to be ashamed, rightly dividing the word of truth" (2 Timothy 2:15)*. Do you realize that the Apostle did not limit it to the Pastor, Priest, or Prophet to do the studying? This is an appeal to every steward, disciple of God.

Here is where you are making the big mistake: you are allowing your leaders to read the Word of God for you. Thus, they have the right to come and tell you what God said, and is saying to you, and you must accept it without questioning. One of the reasons is that you have been taught to see the Minister, Priest, Pastor, Bishop, Apostle, whatever you call them, as super holy, special in the eyes of the Lord, and have developed an intimacy with God that you cannot attain, hence what they say is coming down directly from God. Here is what one of the Prophets himself said under the inspiration of the Spirit: *"And when the people saw what Paul had done, they lifted up their voices, saying in the speech of Lycaonia, The gods are come down to us in the likeness of men. And they called Barnabas, Jupiter; and Paul, Mercurius, because he was the chief speaker. Then the priest of Jupiter, who was before their city, brought oxen and garlands unto the gates, and would have done a sacrifice with the people. Which when the apostles, Barnabas and Paul, heard of, they rent their clothes, and ran in among the people, crying out, and saying, Sirs, why do ye these things? We also are men of like passions with you, and preach unto you that ye should turn from these vanities unto the living God, which made heaven, and earth, and the sea, and all things that are therein"* (Acts 14:11-15). Note, this was a priest doing this. Some of us would do the same thing for some of our spiritual leaders if it were not frowned upon. We do something similar by putting them in the place of God. I met a young lady who wouldn't do or say anything before she asks her Bishop first. This is also our fault, as their spiritual leaders, we behave as though we are God to our congregations. Like the congregation I used to teach their Sunday School, the Pastor had so much control over them that they could not buy, receive, or read that book until their Pastor read and approved it. I had to say to him, teach them the principles you use to evaluate the book and let them decide for themselves. The same Holy Spirit that is guiding you will guide them. It is about control; we need to surrender it to the Holy Spirit, because we cannot lead others into truth. That is the work of the Spirit of God *(John 16:13)*.

You Are Without Excuse

Now you cannot come up with a legitimate reason or excuse why you cannot study: Understand that excuses are those things that stand in place of a lie. With the information age, everything is so easily accessible; this is the opposite of the Dark Ages, when only the Priest could read the Bible because it was written in Latin. This was not the common language of the people. However, you must be very careful, because not all the information you receive is truth. You must examine it against the Word and ask the Holy Spirit to reveal to you if it is truth or not. Then you also must scrutinize your motive for obtaining the information; is it to be used against your fellow humans? Is it so that you can be puffed up and thus feel better than others? Is it to confirm what you already believe? These are impure motives and can therefore lead to self-aggrandizement, self-promotion, and self-glory.

The knowledge of the Word is not enough; you need an understanding of it. Is it true? How does it apply to your life, family, and others? Then you need wisdom on how to apply this knowledge to your life and all that is in your sphere. You cannot use it selfishly or grudgingly, because as God's steward, your responsibility is to advance God's Kingdom.

The opposite is taking place in the world, governments, churches, jobs, homes, and every other group you can find; most are into withholding information. The objective is for control. If you impart it to others, they will begin to experience liberty and thus start to live a fulfilled life. They will no longer be under your control. The Church has been doing this for centuries, keeping its membership poor and obligated to the organization.

In the area of politics, religions have kept their membership in ignorance, and there is no Biblical evidence or basis for it. Life is about politics. The Bible is God's manifesto and constitution. It instructs us about what He wants to do and how He wants His Kingdom's form of government to rule on earth. You need to understand your place in His government and how He wants you to advance His Kingdom.

CHAPTER 5

Separation of Church and State: A Misnomer

This is another lie we have been fed. In the American Constitution, there is no mention of the separation of church and state, which is the ploy of the enemy. I believe his objective is to ensure that true disciples or stewards of God do not get involved in the political process. This would foil the devil's plans because there would be more pushback against the earthly governments and disciples wanting them to be run like the Kingdom government in heaven, even if they were killed in the process, like the early disciples and martyrs. It was never God's or the United States' original plan that the State and the Church be separated. Here is why: there can be no separation of church and state; it is impossible. That is why it is not in the American Constitution. Let us read it and you can see what it says, it is the first amendment: Amendment I. 'Congress shall make no law respecting an establishment of religion, or prohibiting the free exercise thereof; or abridging the freedom of speech, or of the press, or the right of the people peaceably to assemble, and to petition the Government for a redress of grievances.' We need to be reminded of the latter part of the First Amendment in our society today, and how it is being trampled upon.

Here is why I believe it is impossible to separate church and state. In essence, the Church represents our belief system, and the state is defined by the lawmakers. You cannot separate your beliefs from the laws you make. Your laws will be in accordance with your beliefs; thus, it is impossible to separate them. The enemy loves separation and segregation. He has been so effective that he has caused the church to withdraw from discussing politics. The Constitution states that the government should not establish or choose a religion. Neither will it stop anyone from practicing their religion. That is why we have churches of satan, and the government cannot stop them from worshiping. If you elect them, they will make laws according to their beliefs. When we do not get involved in the process, we must take what we get, and we cannot complain. The enemy is the one who is into separation and segregation. We always think we can separate our beliefs in God from our workplace, our business, school, etc. This creates dissonance for us.

God Is A Politician

God is involved in the political system; that is another reason you cannot separate Church and State: God is a politician par excellence. I don't believe politics originated on earth but in heaven. I know that it is creating dissonance for some of you. Don't turn me off; continue reading, and let me make my case based on the Word of God. I know for some of you, it sounds sacrilegious, equating God with politics, which is so vile, detestable, and despicable. The truth is, nothing is wrong with politics; it is impossible to exist without politics, whether you are in a perfect or imperfect environment. Humanity has corrupted the concept of politics. There is nothing wrong with politics; it is like money, business, worship, and prosperity. Man has corrupted them for his own benefit. This does not mean they are corrupt; we use them corruptly.

Let us return to God in heaven, who established His form of government. The Psalmist tells us: *For the kingdom is the Lord's: and he is the governor among the nations" (Psalm 22:28)*. His form of government is a kingdom, and we all will agree that this is a political system. Now, you cannot deny that a governor is a political position. Before you separate God from the rest of us, remember, He created us, and therefore, what we have, we have from Him, the exception being sin, of course.

The Lord has gone even further in the New Testament. God is deeply involved in government and, by extension, politics. Here is what the Apostle Paul tells us in listing some of the gifts: *"And God hath set some in the church, first apostles, secondarily prophets, thirdly teachers, after that miracles, then gifts of healings, helps, governments, diversities of tongues" (1 Corinthians 12:28)*. He has given the gift of politics, so we can know how to run governments. But that is not all, here is God's concept of government and why Church and State cannot be separated. *"Let every soul be subject unto the higher powers. For there is no power but of God: the powers that be are ordained of God. Whosoever therefore resisteth the power, resisteth the ordinance of God: and they that resist shall receive to themselves damnation. For rulers are not a terror to good works, but to the evil. Wilt thou then not be afraid of the power? Do that which is good, and thou shalt have praise of the same: For he is the minister of God to thee for good. But if thou do that which is evil, be afraid; for he beareth not the sword in vain: for he is the minister of God, a revenger to execute wrath upon him that doeth evil" (Romans 13:1-4)*. God calls political leaders His ministers. One reason is to serve God's people. I could not understand why the British referred to their elected representatives as Ministers, such as the Minister of

Finance, Tourism, and Infrastructure, etc. Here is where they got it from; it is Biblical. God calls the politicians His ministers.

Furthermore, the Lord calls upon us to pray for those in authority over us: *"I exhort therefore, that, first of all, supplications, prayers, intercessions, and giving of thanks, be made for all men; For kings, and for all that are in authority; that we may lead a quiet and peaceable life in all godliness and honesty. For this is good and acceptable in the sight of God our Saviour" (1 Timothy 2:1-3)*. Do you realize that God is saying, 'Pray to me about your political leaders'? He is involved in the political process.

I hope you see it from God's perspective and thus get involved not just in voting, but also in considering whether God is calling you to be a politician and make a difference in your community.

A Kingdom is a Form of Governing

Politics originated in heaven, where the Lord established His Kingdom form of government. satan disagreed with God's form of government and decided to establish his own. You see, that is how God created all His children to be involved in politics. So, lucifer created his opposition party to God in heaven. In fact, during his campaigning, he had some success. He was able to convince one-third of the Angels that his party, his form of government, was better than that of God's party. When he was cast out of heaven and came to earth, he continued his campaigning and was able to get Adam and Eve's votes, and they joined his party.

Then the Lord called His candidate, Noah, to campaign for Him, and only eight voted for the Lord, and it seems like all the rest the devil won over to his party. Then the Lord called upon Abraham to campaign on His behalf. What was God's plan: *"Now the Lord had said unto Abram, Get thee out of thy country, and from thy kindred, and from thy father's house, unto a land that I will shew thee: And I will make of thee a great nation, and I will bless thee, and make thy name great; and thou shalt be a blessing: And I will bless them that bless thee, and curse him that curseth thee: and in thee shall all families of the earth be blessed"* (Genesis 12:1-3). Notice what God's plan was: not to create a religion, but to create a nation. Governments and politicians run nations. You will find this throughout the Bible, which is why it is considered a political book. The Lord was not concerned with religion; He is more interested in nation-building. You will recognize the same thing in *Genesis 17:5-6, 15-16*, when He changed Abram and Sarai's names; it was about nations, kings, and kingdoms, all related to politics. Nations must, out of necessity, operate in the context of politics. Actually, once you have people, you will automatically have politics, whether you want it or not. So, the Church and State cannot be separated; they are interconnected.

Let us take it further, every nation or kingdom needs a judicial system so that the people can experience justice. In establishing Israel as a nation, while it was being formed, God used Jethro, Moses' father-in-law to help him set up the judicial system in Exodus 18:19-21: *"Hearken now unto my voice, I will give thee counsel, and God shall be with thee: Be thou for the people to God-ward, that thou mayest bring the causes unto God: And thou shalt teach them ordinances and laws, and shalt shew them the way wherein they must walk, and the work that they must do. Moreover thou shalt provide out of all the people able men, such as fear God, men of truth, hating covetousness; and place such over them, to be rulers of thousands, and rulers of hundreds, rulers of fifties, and rulers of tens."* Note that it was, and still is, the political ruler who appoints the judges in many nations. There is no doubt that Moses was the political ruler of the nation of Israel. He did the appointing of judges. This is a similar justice system that is being emulated worldwide. Just as today, they were trained and, based on their giftedness, were to be judges over thousands, hundreds, fifties, and rulers of tens, according to their gifts and abilities.

Every nation or kingdom needs a health system so that its people can experience good health. Again, for the nation of Israel, the Lord helped Moses establish the health laws in the book of Leviticus. Politics is a subject we cannot avoid. What is politics? Again, to me, it is a group of people elected or selected from the community to create policies that will benefit the majority of the people, allowing us to live together in harmony and achieve success. And find out ways to help those in the minority.

You say nation-building was only in the Old Testament. Let me show you that the Lord is still involved in nation-building, thus it includes politics. Let us see what Peter tells us: *"But ye are a chosen generation, a royal priesthood, a holy nation, a peculiar people; that ye should shew forth the praises of him who hath called you out of darkness into his marvellous light"* (1 Peter 2:9). Notice, there is the same concept of a nation. The Lord keeps reminding us He is the same yesterday, today, and forever *(Hebrews 13:8)*.

The Difficulties Between Church and State

These are difficulties created by man, not by God. One of the confusions is that someone said there should be a separation of church and state, but you haven't thought it through. Furthermore, it is repeated and written over and over, and you believe that makes it true. No, it does not. I understand the context in which it was made—that no religion should dictate what the government does. However, this has been taken out of context and to the extreme of the church members playing no part in the state. Hence, anything that has any association with the church must be gotten rid of, so the Ten Commandments are taken down in every government building, prayer is no longer acceptable in schools, the nativity scene must go, and the Bible must not be a part of our political decisions. That is where all the righteous laws came from, God's Manifesto and Constitution.

Here is my question to you: Have you consulted God's Word to see what He says about the subject of politics? If you are His obedient steward, then you will consult His Word for the Truth. Yes, this might be true for disobedient stewards, but it does not apply to God's obedient stewards.

Let Us Examine This Statement

Who is the church? According to the New Testament, you are known in Greek as the ecclesia, the called-out ones. This does not refer to the physical building, such as the temple or the church, but to the people who inhabit it. It has always been about people; in the beginning, it was to the literal Israelites, and now it is to spiritual Israelites *(Galatians 3:26-29)*. It's all about the people. Here is what the Apostle Paul says: *"What? Know ye not that your body is the temple of the Holy Ghost which is in you, which ye have of God, and ye are not your own? For ye are bought with a price: Therefore, glorify God in your body, and in your spirit, which are God's"* (1 Corinthians 6:19-20, see also 1 Corinthians 3:16-17). The Bible goes so far as to call you the temple of God. Why, because God has always been about His people, not about buildings. Jesus clarifies this truth when speaking to the woman at the well, an outcast by society, but one whom Jesus loved. This is what He said to her: *"But the hour cometh, and now is, when the true worshippers shall worship the Father in spirit and in truth: for the Father seeketh such to worship him. God is a Spirit: and they that worship him must worship him in spirit and in truth"* (John 4:23-24). So that worship is not confined to a building, it is about The Person who is concerned about His people. Therefore, you need to learn to worship God at all times, 24/7. So that if you are a Politician, you must learn to worship God as a Politician while you are campaigning. If you are a Judge, you must learn to worship Him as a Judge while carrying out your role and responsibilities. If you are a Janitor, you also must seek to worship him as a Janitor 24/7, or any other vocation to which God has called you. (For more details, see the books: "We Were Made To Worship God 24/7! Is It Possible?" and "It Is Possible To Worship God 24/7"). Thus, you cannot be separated from the state.

Furthermore, how can you separate church and state when the government is a part of the state, and the state is comprised of the people? I know they mean that no Church should be determining what the State should be doing. However, the Church has misinterpreted this and taken it to another level, encouraging its members not to get involved in the political process; some agree that one should vote. They are encouraged to stay away otherwise. This is not Biblical. Furthermore, you are making sure that God's people are not running, and you are asking them to vote for non-believers whose beliefs are contrary to God's. How does this make sense?

The separation of Church and State, technically speaking, is a misnomer because they cannot be separated, especially if you are a steward or disciple of Jesus. Many of the same individuals who are in politics are also involved in the church. You cannot separate your beliefs from who you are, or else you are a hypocrite. Your beliefs fuel your decision-making. Here is an example of what I mean: the Three Hebrew Boys in Babylon. They were in a foreign country, and King Nebuchadnezzar wanted them to bow down and worship the image he had built. This was both political and religious, the state and the church: *"Shadrach, Meshach, and Abednego, answered and said to the king, we are not careful to answer thee in this matter. If it be so, our God whom we serve is able to deliver us from the burning fiery furnace, and he will deliver us out of thine hand, O king. But if not, be it known unto thee, O king, that we will* not serve thy gods, nor worship the golden image which thou hast set up. Then was Nebuchadnezzar full of fury, and the form of his visage was changed against [them]: therefore he spake, and commanded that they should heat the furnace seven times more than it was wont to be heated. And he commanded the most mighty men that were in his army to bind [them], and to cast them into the burning fiery furnace. Then these men were bound...and cast into the midst of the burning fiery furnace. Therefore, because the king's commandment was urgent, and the furnace exceeding hot, the flames of the fire slew those men that took up Shadrach, Meshach, and Abednego. And these three men fell down bound into the midst of the fiery furnace. Then the king was astonished, and rose up in haste, and spake, and said unto his counsellors, Did not we cast three men bound into the midst of the fire? They answered and said unto the king, True, O king. He answered and said, Lo, I see four men loose, walking in the midst of the fire, and they have no hurt; and the form of the fourth is like the Son of God" (Daniel 3:16-25). For these men, there could not be a separation of church and state, because they worked for the State and their belief system affected how they responded to the state. When the state violates the steward of Jesus' beliefs, he would rather die than succumb to the state's authority. This is what many Christians want to escape. People are afraid to die for the Truth, Jesus. So, it is easier to stay away and avoid persecution. A disciple or steward of God will not avoid and or be afraid.

The Results of Trying to Separate

Because you try to separate Church and State, you suffer from schizophrenia, thus, an identity crisis. You cannot practice something in one area and not practice it in all areas of your life. You are a holistic person; therefore, what you practice in one area will automatically carry over to others. For example, if you are accustomed to lying, you will not just lie in one area. If you are a thief, you will find new ways and places to steal. You see, that is how you were made, to be fruitful, multiply, fill the earth, subdue, and have dominion *(Genesis 1:28)*. It does not matter if it is positive or negative. You cannot live a disconnected, isolated, or segmented life. If you are, examine your motives. There are some benefits you are trying to derive, and you are consistently coming up short. That is one of the reasons why you feel unfulfilled, unsatisfied, frustrated, angry, and torn. So, you cannot separate church and state.

God designed you to be a whole being; everything is integrated and cannot be isolated, compartmentalized, or segmented. If you do, you will eventually get physically sick. Most of the time, doctors will not be able to diagnose the sickness because it is psychosomatic. All kinds of sickness occur, mental, social, psychological, physical, financial, spiritual, and other maladies. You were not designed to live this way.

Why You Cannot Separate Church and State?

How can you separate church and state when God is the one who sets up kings and takes them down? *"And he changeth the times and the seasons: he removeth kings, and setteth up kings: he giveth wisdom unto the wise, and knowledge to them that know understanding" (Daniel 2:21)*. This means that God is involved in the political process. Not only kings, presidents, chief ministers, politicians, CEOs, and COOs. Notice how He does it, by giving them knowledge, wisdom, and understanding. That means you must be involved so that God can use you to accomplish His purposes. Thus, as His obedient steward, you must be involved in politics. If God is involved, it means that, as His disciple and steward, so must you. You are His representative here on earth, which is why He made you in His image. Remember, it is the enemy who is trying extremely hard to keep you out of what God wants you to be involved in.

CHAPTER 6

The Role of Pastors, Prophets, Priests, and Ministers

Here is what I found when reading the Word of God. This group is among the first to speak out against those in authority, regardless of the form the government takes, whether it is a democracy, a monarchy, or a dictatorship.

Speak Out Against the Wrong

I know from personal experience that this is a tremendous challenge because every time you do, you are literally putting your life on the line. It therefore means you should be prepared to die, if necessary. This makes many afraid. You will be called all kinds of names; however, you are in good company, for that is what they did to Jesus. He was called a glutton, a wine bibber, a friend of sinners (Luke 7:34). If you can't deal with this soft reaction, how would you be able to face death? You cannot hinder persecution; this is what the Word of God says: *"Yea, and all that will live godly in Christ Jesus shall suffer persecution" (2 Timothy 3:12)*. It is inevitable; therefore, you must learn to embrace it. There are times when confrontation must be handled privately and other times when it must be handled publicly. The Spirit of

God will reveal to you when and what is the appropriate time to do so.

Here is what we don't understand: when we speak out, it is our testimony; we are testifying. How important are our testimonies? Let us listen to what the Apostle John tells us from His experience: *"And I heard a loud voice saying in heaven, Now is come salvation, and strength, and the kingdom of our God, and the power of his Christ: for the accuser of our brethren is cast down, which accused them before our God day and night. And they overcame him by the blood of the Lamb, and by the word of their testimony; and they loved not their lives unto the death"* (Revelations 12:11-12). Do you realize that along with the blood of Jesus, our testimonies are what help us to overcome the enemy, and most importantly, we are not afraid to die, because it prepares us to face death? Now, the only way this is possible is that God has given us salvation when we accept Him as our Lord and Savior (see Appendix 1). The strength that you need to testify is already within you (2 Peter 1:3), and you have the backing of the entire Kingdom of God. Furthermore, you have the power of Jesus accompanying you. Therefore, you are not afraid of the accuser of the brethren. You will testify of the Lord in the land of the living. What will your testimonies be about? The Psalmist tells you: *"All thy works shall praise thee, O Lord; and thy saints shall bless thee. They shall speak of the glory of thy kingdom, and talk of thy power; To make known to the sons of men his mighty acts, and the glorious majesty of his kingdom. Thy kingdom is an everlasting kingdom, and thy dominion endureth throughout all generations. The Lord upholdeth all that fall, and raiseth up all those that be bowed down"* (Psalm 145:10-14). All this will happen so that those listening can know and understand this awesome God, accept Him, and become one of His disciples.

Here is the warning that John gives: *"Therefore rejoice, ye heavens, and ye that dwell in them. Woe to the inhabiters of the earth* and of the sea! for the devil is come down unto you, having great wrath, because he knoweth that he hath but a short time" (Revelation 12:13). Yes, we can rejoice for those souls who turn their lives over to the Lord; however, we must be aware that the devil is present. He knows that his time is short, and therefore, he is ramping up his destruction and death. He wants many souls to be destroyed with him.

Let us examine the roles of some Pastors, Prophets, Priests, and Ministers.

Moses

Let us begin with the Prophet Moses, who is a typical example of how we respond when God calls us to speak out against the evils in our society. God called upon him to confront the King of Egypt because of what he was doing to the children of Israel. Here is how Moses himself described it: *"Now therefore, behold, the cry of the children of Israel is come unto me: and I have also seen the oppression wherewith the Egyptians oppress them. Come now therefore, and I will send thee unto Pharaoh, that thou mayest bring forth my people, the children of Israel, out of Egypt"* (Exodus 3:7-10). This is what God calls His politicians to do: speak out against the evils of society, those who are taking advantage of His children.

However, like Moses, we argue with God and find excuse after excuse why he did not qualify for the task to which God was calling him. First, he said, who am I that I should deliver the children of Israel out of Egypt (Exodus 3 & 4). In other words, he was saying to God, 'I am a nobody; all I do is look after sheep.' His next excuse was that the people would not believe You really sent me. When the Lord answered those excuses, Moses said, okay Lord, when I go, who should I say sent me, and God gave that decisive pronouncement of who He is, 'I am that I am.' He was saying to Moses and to you, I will be to you who and what you want me to be. That still was not enough. God then performed some miracles before his very eyes: his rod turned to a snake, his hand became leprous, and then it was whole again. Yet, he comes up with a final excuse: I cannot go because I stammer, and God asked him who made his mouth and his tongue.

He finally goes, and things get worse for the Israelites, but they believed the Lord had visited them through Moses. Then God said this to him, and I find this answer fascinating. This is the first time I realize it was on September 4, 2017. I have taught from this passage numerous times. *"And the Lord said unto Moses, See, I have made thee a god to Pharaoh: and Aaron thy brother shall be thy prophet" (Exodus 7:1).* This is one of the titles God gives to His faithful stewards, the title of small g, god (see the book, "Kingdom Stewardship and The Titles"). God was saying I make you like me. You are made in my image, and I will even give your brother as your prophet. That is and has been God's desire.

The reason why Moses, you, and I have difficulty with going is that it is a challenge; the task is bigger than us, we are incapable of accomplishing it in our own strength, and we need the help of the Lord. And so, we are overwhelmed and unsure of the outcome. Thus, you believe you will be defeated. What makes it more challenging is that he will give you some of the information, but never all of it. You must learn to walk by faith. Moses had to go to Pharaoh 10 times before he let the Israelites go. You must be ready to do what God says. What increases the intensity is that the same people you are helping will turn on you and accuse you of wanting to kill them. *"Is not this the word that we did tell thee in Egypt, saying, Let us alone, that we may serve the Egyptians? For it had been better for us to serve the Egyptians, than that we should die in the wilderness" (Exodus 14:11).* But you must learn to push through, because it is God's assignment He has given you.

Jesus

He is our ultimate example in every aspect of life and has consistently spoken out against the ills of society. He was constantly opposing those who were wrong and trying to oppress others. For example, the woman caught in adultery they brought to Jesus because, according to the Law, she was to be stoned. This was a political move. But they were deceitful and did not bring the man with whom she was committing adultery. Here is what the Bible says: *"And the man that committeth adultery with another man's wife, even he that committeth adultery with his neighbour's wife, the adulterer and the adulteress shall surely be put to death"* (**Leviticus 20:10**). Jesus confronted them.

There were times He called the leaders whitened sepulchers, hypocrites, generation of vipers, or snakes. In Matthew 23 alone, Jesus pronounced eight woes against those who should have been the spiritual leaders of the day, the Scribes and Pharisees, and he called them hypocrites *(Verses 13-16, 23, 25, 27, 29)*. They were not fulfilling their responsibilities. Let us look at just one of the woes in verses 27-28: *"Woe unto you, scribes and Pharisees, hypocrites! for ye are like unto whited sepulchres, which indeed appear beautiful outward, but are within full of dead men's bones, and of all uncleanness. Even so ye also outwardly appear righteous unto men, but within ye are full of hypocrisy and iniquity."* These were the spiritual leaders He was speaking to, calling them out, and addressing their hypocrisy, as they appeared pious on the outside but rotten on the inside. As a leader and one of His faithful stewards, you must examine your life to ensure that these woes do not apply to you. In addition, if you can call out the religious leaders, then it is also okay to call out the political leaders.

How Did Jesus Address the Politicians?

When Jesus was brought bound before Herod, he tried to treat Him like a circus clown. He wanted Him to perform some miracles, and Jesus refused. Then he questioned Him, and Jesus declined to answer. I believe because He knew it would not have made a difference, so why waste His breath. He needed that energy to carry the weight of the cross and dying on it.

When He was brought before the Governor, Pilate, Jesus was also questioned by him. Pilate asked Him if He was the King of the Jews; He said, 'You said it.' When He asked Jesus about the accusations that the Jews brought against Him, He did not answer a word. This was Pilate's response: *"Then saith Pilate unto him, Speakest thou not unto me? Knowest thou not that I have power to crucify thee, and have power to release thee?"* (John 19:10). Listen to Jesus' response, *"Jesus answered, Thou couldest have no power at all against me, except it were given thee from above: therefore he that delivered me unto thee hath the greater sin"* (John 19:11). You don't have to respond to everything; that's why you need the Holy Spirit to instruct you on what to say and when not to say it. Luke declares: *"And when they bring you unto the synagogues, and unto magistrates, and powers, take ye no thought how or what thing ye shall answer, or what ye shall say: For the Holy Ghost shall teach you in the same hour what ye ought to say"* (Luke 12:11-12). When God gives you your assignment, He will be thorough in preparing you to carry it out.

John the Baptist

When Herod married his brother's wife, John the Baptist confronted him and told him it was wrong. Here is what Matthew wrote: *"For Herod had laid hold on John, and bound him, and put him in prison for Herodias' sake, his brother Philip's wife. For John said unto him, it is not lawful for thee to have her. And when he would have put him to death, he feared the multitude, because they counted him as a prophet"* (Matthew 14:3-5). John, who was the forerunner of Jesus, did not play and was not afraid of the authorities; they were scared of him. That is why he was beheaded. He was not afraid of the King, because as God's faithful steward, he knew the King of kings. The Lord is also calling upon us all, however, here more specifically to call out those in authority, regardless of whether they are kings, presidents, elected officials, spiritual leaders, or civic leaders. The good news is you don't have to worry about what you need to say: *"Behold, I send you forth as sheep in the midst of wolves: be ye therefore wise as serpents, and harmless as doves. But beware of men: for they will deliver you up to the councils, and they will scourge you in their synagogues; And ye shall be brought before governors and kings for my sake, for a testimony against them and the Gentiles. But when they deliver you up, take no thought how or what ye shall speak: for it shall be given you in that same hour what ye shall speak. For it is not ye that speak, but the Spirit of your Father which speaketh in you"* (Matthew 10:16-20). Whether you want to confront the authorities, you will have to, because you will be brought before them. They will beat you, say all manner of evil against you, ridicule, malign, and call you all kinds of names. Remember, you are there to testify to the goodness of the Lord; you are there as a witness for God. Just as Moses, Jesus wants us to be wise as serpents and harmless as doves, not worrying about what we need to say, because in that same hour, He will provide the words that are not ours but His. Of course, these are much more powerful because His word is alive and can give life to the hearer, if they want to accept it.

A Man of God

This is a fascinating story in the Old Testament: *"And, behold, there came a man of God out of Judah by the word of the LORD unto Bethel: and (King) Jeroboam stood by the altar to burn incense. And he cried against the altar in the word of the LORD, and said, O altar, altar, thus saith the LORD; Behold, a child shall be born unto the house of David, Josiah by name; and upon thee shall he offer the priests of the high places that burn incense upon thee, and men's bones shall be burnt upon thee. And he gave a sign the same day, saying, This is the sign which the* LORD *hath spoken; Behold, the altar shall be rent, and the ashes that are upon it shall be poured out. And it came to pass, when King Jeroboam heard the saying of the man of God, which had cried against the altar in Bethel, that he put forth his hand from the altar, saying, Lay hold on him. And his hand, which he put forth against him, dried up, so that he could not pull it in again to him. The altar also was rent, and the ashes poured out from the altar, according to the sign which the man of God had given by the word of the* LORD. *And the king answered and said unto the man of God, Intreat now the face of the* LORD *thy God, and pray for me, that my hand may be restored to me. And the man of God besought the* LORD, *and the king's hand was restored to him again, and became as it was before"* (1 Kings 13:1-6). The man of God was not afraid of the King. He followed God's instructions to confront the King of Israel. The King was humbled, and the man of God had to pray for him to restore his withered hand. When I used to read this story, I wondered why this man of God was not given a title, prophet, priest, or Levite. That is how we think. It simply says, 'man of God,' which means this could be any one of God's obedient stewards and disciples. It is not just left up to those in leadership. You have to listen to God when He gives you your instructions to confront whoever He instructs you to engage. This man of God went to the King of Israel, a political figure, and told him that what he was doing was wrong, and this was done in the temple, where others were present. You cannot see wrong, wickedness, abuse, and God calls you to speak out against it, and you refuse. This means you are disobedient.

Jonah

This book is a captivating one, as God sends His prophet to Nineveh to declare to the King and the people of Nineveh that if they do not repent, God will destroy the entire nation. These were some of the cruelest people on the face of the earth. They had mastered the art of torture. Remember that Jonah did not want to go, and here is why: *"But it displeased Jonah exceedingly, and he was very angry. And he prayed unto the LORD, and said, I pray thee, O LORD, was not this my saying, when I was yet in my country? Therefore, I fled before unto Tarshish: for I knew that thou art a gracious God, and merciful, slow to anger, and of great kindness, and repentest thee of the evil"* (Jonah 4:1-2). He continues: *"And Jonah began to enter into the city a day's journey, and he cried, and said, Yet forty days, and Nineveh shall be overthrown. So the people of Nineveh believed God, and proclaimed a fast, and put on sackcloth, from the greatest of them even to the least. For the word came unto the king of Nineveh, and he arose from his throne, and he laid his robe from him, and covered himself with sackcloth, and sat in ashes. And he caused it to be proclaimed and published through Nineveh by the decree of the king and his nobles, saying, Let neither man nor beast, taste any thing: let them not feed, nor drink water: But let man and beast be covered with sackcloth, and cry mightily unto God: yea, let them turn everyone from his evil way, and from the violence that is in their hands. Who can tell if God will turn and repent, and turn away from his fierce anger, that we perish not? And God saw their works, that they turned from their evil way; and God repented of the evil, that he had said that he would do unto them; and he did it not"* (Jonah 3:4-19). Thankfully, all of Nineveh, from the King right down to the most common person, heeded Jonah's warning, and the nation was saved. He confronted all, including the King. This is why it is so important to carry out God's instructions of confronting those in leadership.

You never know who will repent and be saved, as Jonah did; you can be saving an entire nation.

Nathan The Prophet

When David, the King of Israel, took another man's wife and made her pregnant. God called upon his servant Nathan to confront King David over the wrong he had done to this family. The prophet began with a story of two men: one was rich and the other was poor. The rich man had many sheep, yet he took the poor man's only lamb and killed it. This was King David's response: *"And David's anger was greatly kindled against the man; and he said to Nathan, As the LORD liveth, the man that hath done this thing shall surely die: And he shall restore the lamb fourfold, because he did this thing, and because he had no pity"* (2 Samuel 12:5-6). He did not realize he was referring to himself. This was the prophet's response: *"And Nathan said to David, Thou art the man. Thus saith the Lord God of Israel, I anointed thee king over Israel, and I delivered thee out of the hand of Saul"* (2 Samuel 12:7). As you can see, this was done privately.

Samuel

When King Saul disobeyed the voice of God, He called upon His servant Samuel to confront the King: *"And Samuel said, Hath the LORD as great delight in burnt offerings and sacrifices, as in obeying the voice of the LORD? Behold, to obey is better than sacrifice, and to hearken than the fat of rams. For rebellion is as the sin of witchcraft, and stubbornness is as iniquity and idolatry. Because thou hast rejected the word of the LORD, he hath also rejected thee from being king. And Saul said unto Samuel, I have sinned: for I have transgressed the commandment of the LORD, and thy words: because I feared the people, and obeyed their voice* (1 Samuel 15:22-24). From all indications, this seems to have been done publicly. As we have seen, there will be times when we must confront privately and other times publicly; the Holy Spirit will instruct you when to do so.

The Priests

Here is what I find fascinating, the Priests in Nehemiah's day were the first to begin the process of rebuilding the walls of Jerusalem: *"Then Eliashib the high priest rose up with his brethren the priests, and they builded the sheep gate; they sanctified it, and set up the doors of it; even unto the tower of Meah they sanctified it, unto the tower of Hananeel. And next unto him builded the men of Jericho. And next to them builded Zaccur the son of Imri"* (Nehemiah 3:1-2). They did not wait for others to begin; they jumped right in. This is what the Lord wants us to do: when there is a job to be done, it doesn't matter what it is; once you hear from God, go to work, and He will provide all that you need.

CHAPTER 7

Jesus and Politics

Why Didn't Jesus Bring Another Religion?

First, there were already too many religions in His day. Thus, there would have been competition between them, like there is today. Jesus' objective is oneness, not religion. Religion creates chaos, division, and isolation because it is man's search for the Kingdom of God, and religious people are not aware of this truth. Thus, religion will never be able to accomplish its purpose because you do not know what it is. Whenever you do not understand the purpose of anything, you will abuse and misuse it. Just like the Scripture points out: *"For ye have heard of my conversation in time past in the Jews' religion, how that beyond measure I persecuted the church of God, and wasted it" (Galatians 1:13)*. Paul was a member of the Pharisees' religion. He used it to persecute the obedient stewards of God's kingdom; by the way, his power and instructions came from his church's government, not from above.

Second, Jesus understood that whoever controls the philosophies, laws, values, and morals controls the culture. Religion does not control society; it doesn't and cannot legislate, nor can it create values or morals for the nation. Politicians and the government do. Communities are a collection of families; from these, we derive our society, which is how we interact with one another. Then we have a nation which is a collection of communities. Whoever controls the community controls the nation; thus, the government controls the nation or country, and it is consequently referred to as a national government.

How does the government create a culture? It begins with a belief system; the only way to change the world is with the introduction of a government. This is precisely what Jesus did by introducing Heaven's form of government. As His faithful steward, you must understand how God's Kingdom government operates.

Why We Are In Trouble Politically

The reason why our nations are in moral crises is because the people of God, I am not talking about nominal Christians, like the Scribes and Pharisees in Jesus' day. But faithful stewards, disciples of Jesus who are living out their faith, and are stepping up to the plate politically. These are only a few examples, stemming from a misunderstanding of politics and what God expects from His genuine stewards.

What was one of Jesus' purposes for coming to Earth? Here is what the prophet Isaiah confirms: *"For unto us a child is born, unto us a son is given: and the government shall be upon his shoulder: and his name shall be called Wonderful, Counsellor, The mighty God, The everlasting Father, The Prince of Peace" (Isaiah 9:6-7)*. Hence, Jesus came to reestablish His Kingdom form of government. The same one He created when He formed the earth. It was a Kingdom in which He wanted man to rule on earth as He ruled in Heaven. Jesus confirms this in the Disciple's Prayer, when He prayed that what was happening in heaven would happen here on earth (Matthew 6:10).

Why Did Jesus Bring A Government?

This is a question you need to answer. What does the Bible say? *"And God hath set some in the church, first apostles, secondarily prophets, thirdly teachers, after that miracles, then gifts of healings, helps, governments, diversities of tongues" (1 Corinthians 12:28).* As you can see, one of the gifts that God gives to His people is the gift of governments. Many people are unaware of this, which is why I mentioned earlier the importance of learning to teach and understand everything within the context of the Kingdom. Since we are not involved in politics, this truth is often overlooked, resulting in disconnection and isolation.

Politics is not as bad as the world has made it to be. God is not afraid of government; neither should you. You see that the Godhead wants what is happening in heaven to also happen on earth. In other words, Heaven wants to colonize Earth, which is a political process. As you read in Isaiah 9:6, the government shall be upon Jesus' shoulders. Verse 7 states that His government will increase and will not come to an end. Jesus' form of government is here, growing, and will last forever. You can either be a part of it, or you will be crushed by it, when the Stone in Daniel 2 is cut out without hands and destroys the Kingdoms of this world and their governments.

Furthermore, the Government is the most powerful force on earth right now, not any religion. Why, you ask? Because they make the laws, create the values or morals for any country, not the church people. Thus, the Government is essential to us all. Interestingly, everyone wants to be part of the government and is preoccupied with it, as we are now.

What is so Important About Government?

What did Jesus come as? *"Pilate therefore said unto him, Art thou a king then? Jesus answered, Thou sayest that I am a king. To this end was I born, and for this cause came I into the world, that I should bear witness unto the truth. Everyone that is of the truth heareth my voice" (John 18:37).* He came as a King, and Pilate confirmed this truth. A king is a political office responsible for governing a people. If Jesus were a King, there had to be a Kingdom; you cannot have a King without a Kingdom. The King has the authority within Himself. Unlike elected officials, they cannot carry their authority with them wherever they go. Thus, the Kingdom was present wherever Jesus was, just as it is with any King.

What are some other characteristics of a King? The King is never elected; you become a king by birth or usurpation, not by election. The King's word is law; it is unchangeable, always current, never out of date. Hence, the Word of God is His constitution. Unlike a democracy, no one can question the word of the King. That is why you cannot question the Word; it is the King's Word and is always present, not outdated.

These are some of the reasons Jesus came as a King, because religion does not and cannot legislate. He did not bring a new doctrine, but He gave you dominion over the earth. Jesus did not give new rituals to replace the ones that He and the Jews created. Instead, He restored kingship —stewardship of that which was shown in the beginning. As valuable and powerful as democracy is, Jesus did not bring that; instead, He brought the kingdom He prepared from the foundation of the world *(Matthew 25:34).* Finally, He did not bring a religion because religion does not create culture, laws, values, or morals; government does.

What Jesus Wants to Accomplish Through His Government?

He says in the Disciples' Prayer: *"Thy kingdom come, Thy will be done in earth, as it is in heaven" (Matthew 6:10)*. One of the reasons for Jesus' coming was to bring the culture of heaven to the earth. He wants the earth to be filled with heaven's laws, morals, values, and belief systems. So that what is going on in heaven will be going on here on earth. That is colonization. This is how it is done, through culture and influence. When you look at the Islands that the British colonized, for example, they did not force us to drink tea, drive on the left side of the road, or wear jackets and ties in 90-degree weather. All England did was send a representative, usually a governor from the Mother country, to make sure that what was happening in England was happening in those conquered territories. The laws passed in England also became laws in those countries. Thus, the culture of England became the culture of her territories.

That is what God has done: first, Jesus came, and now the Holy Spirit is the Governor or representative from Heaven; all His disciples make up His colony. It is our responsibility to make Earth as close to heaven as possible. God wants His philosophy to become policy, His laws to become the standards for His Earthly Kingdom. He knows that His laws will produce the same values that are in Heaven. These values then create the morality that should be present in His Kingdom, thereby producing a culture fit for a King living in the Kingdom of the King of Kings.

What Kind of Government Are You Looking For?

Isaiah most eloquently describes it: *"For unto us a child is born, unto us a son is given: and the government shall be upon his shoulder: and his name shall be called Wonderful, Counsellor, The mighty God, The everlasting Father, The Prince of Peace" (Isaiah 9:6)*.

Everybody is looking for a government, not just any kind, you want one for which everyone is searching. One that possesses the characteristics that Jesus came to establish. You want one that is wonderful, provides sound counsel, mighty, to solve all your problems in life, to provide you with peace. That is, a personal government, one that has your best interest at heart, cares about you, and is concerned about you.

These are some of what you look for in your government; it is a very powerful entity, one of the world's greatest needs. Every nation, country, and island spends all its resources on government. And thus, deep down, you know that your life is dependent upon it. Your government sets the kind of lifestyle you live by passing laws. Yes, some lobbyists help influence the laws that are passed. However, suppose your representatives in government allow lobbyists to persuade and influence them. In that case, it is because they are benefiting financially, sexually, or access to power, etc, or it has become their philosophy and way of thinking. No private citizen, no matter how rich, no church, no matter how big or influential, can pass any law; only the representatives in Government can. Of course, some can be paid to vote against your interests. Your responsibility is to vote them out of office.

Do not let anyone fool you; morality can be legislated, as every law is morally coded. Like, if they lower the age for consensual sex or for gays to get married. This affects everyone morally. Hence, you want Heaven's Government here on earth; it is the best you will ever find.

What Is the Meaning of These Titles?

Let us examine them; they are found in Isaiah 9:6:

Wonderful—this is what you are looking for. You want a wonderful spouse, children, job, church, cars, and especially the news. You wish these and other things in your life were wonderful too. With the coming of Jesus, He is the Wonderful that you are looking for and need. You become a wonderful steward for God and for those around you.

Counselor—because almost nothing in your life is wonderful, you need someone to help you experience the wonderful, and so Jesus is your counselor. You can communicate with Him at any time, day or night. You don't have to go through a secretary. He will help you through any problem, challenge, emotion, persecution, it does not matter what it is: *"For in that He himself hath suffered being tempted, He is able to succour them that are tempted"* **(Hebrews 2:18)**. *"Wherefore he is able also to save them to the uttermost that come unto God by him, seeing he ever liveth to make intercession for them"* **(Hebrews 7:25)**.

How does Jesus work as your counselor? Since He does not come down Himself, He has gifted some people as counselors: *"For, when we came into Macedonia, our flesh had no rest, but we were troubled on every side; without were fightings, within were fears. Nevertheless God, that comforteth those that are cast down, comforted us by the coming of Titus"* (2 Corinthians 7:5-6). He uses people to help with your problems. You become a steward who counsels.

Mighty God—As a created being, you are always searching for your Creator, like adopted children have a strong urge to search for their biological parents. If you have your parents, you are searching for a superhero. Notice that they do not come from Earth, but always from a different planet. They always have superpowers because you don't just want any God, you want a mighty God. You will now introduce Him to others.

Everlasting Father—Your parents are fallible and make many mistakes, and so you are searching for a perfect Father. Because your parents died or will die, you are looking for a Father who is not subject to death, one who will live forever. Especially, since you cannot, even though you were created to live forever

(Ecclesiastes 3:11 NIV). As a steward, you become a father to the fatherless.

Prince of Peace—With the entrance of sin, our greatest desire is for peace: *"But the wicked are like the troubled sea, when it cannot rest, whose waters cast up mire and dirt" (Isaiah 57:20).* Your King is Peace. God, knowing this, gave Jesus as one of His titles, Prince of Peace. Hence, when the angels proclaimed Jesus' birth, announced: *"Glory to God in the highest, and on earth peace, good will toward men" (Luke 2:14).* The peace He gives is different, *"Peace I leave with you, my peace I give unto you: not as the world giveth, give I unto you. Let not your heart be troubled, neither let it be afraid" (John 14:27).* As His steward, you personify this peace. Like Jesus, you are calm in crises; you have learned to rely on God.

Jesus came and brought all these and more in the form of His Kingdom government. Eden is being restored—the Kingdom of God is Eden restored. In other words, what was intended originally is being restored to man.

Why Such Ideal Titles?

Do you notice the lofty titles and qualities of this divinely endowed King? (Isaiah 9:6). As we have examined them, you see that this is the kind of government for which you are seeking. King Jesus brought this type of government just for you. Because of sin, you need the attributes that go along with these titles to survive in the Kingdom that God prepared for you.

First, Jesus had to die to redeem you from the curse of sin. Before this, He had to show you how to live in a world that is full of sin. To reveal to you His Kingdom form of government and how He will help you in your daily living to be victorious as His king, steward, and disciple. You must understand that government and peace are not tangible. They cannot be seen. So, what Jesus came to establish is not yet physical. It is because of this that you have difficulty accepting what God says, since they are not physical. Remember what Jesus said to Pilate about His Kingdom: *"My kingdom is not of this world: if my kingdom were of this world, then would my servants fight, that I should not be delivered to the Jews: but now is my kingdom not from hence"* (John 18:36). As His obedient steward, you will begin to become like the King of kings and behave like Him. You will begin to take on the characteristics of these titles, *Wonderful, Counsellor, The Mighty God, The Everlasting Father, The Prince of Peace*, daily, and begin to rule just like Him.

How Will Jesus' Government Increase?

Continuing in Isaiah: *"Of the increase of his government and peace there shall be no end, upon the throne of David, and upon his kingdom, to order it, and to establish it with judgment and with justice from henceforth even forever"* (Isaiah 9:7). Jesus' government is going to increase in the same manner that it was going to grow in the Kingdom He prepared for Adam and Eve. What was His instructions to them: *"And God blessed them, and God said unto them, be fruitful, and multiply, and replenish the earth, and subdue it: and have dominion over the fish of the sea, and over the fowl of the air, and over every living thing that moveth upon the earth"* (Genesis 1:28). There was and is going to be a gradual increase of Eden into the rest of the world. In like manner, His government and peace are right now being fruitful; it has begun to multiply, and it will eventually fill the earth. It is subduing everything in its path and will ultimately have dominion over the entire Earth. Nothing or no one can hinder its progress. That is why you need to know the King, understand His Kingdom, and be His faithful steward: because even today the Kingdom of God's government and peace is increasing, and if you are not a part of it, then you are a part of the Kingdom of satan, and hell is prepared for him and you (Matthew 25:41).

Do not be fooled; you might not be hearing about God's Kingdom government, but that does not mean it is not increasing.

Where is This Going to Take Place

How do you know that it is a Kingdom form of government that Jesus came to establish? Where will all this take place? On the throne of David. Remember, this prophecy began to be fulfilled with the birth of Jesus. Here is what the Angel told Mary: *"And, behold, thou shalt conceive in thy womb, and bring forth a son, and shalt call his name Jesus. He shall be great, and shall be called the Son of the Highest: and the Lord God shall give unto him the throne of his father David: And he shall reign over the house of Jacob forever; and of his kingdom there shall be no end"* (Luke 1:31-33). The Angel confirms the prophecy made by Isaiah, that Jesus would come to reestablish His Kingdom Government, which He first created for Adam and Eve. The good news is, this has already begun. It was and is already here, *"Thy Kingdom come, thy will be done on earth as it is in heaven"* (Matthew 6:10). The Kingdom can only come if it already exists.

Take note that judgment and justice for which you are searching will exist throughout eternity. Injustice and corrupt judgment are what produce the downfall of all Kingdoms. How are you reigning as His king and steward? Is there righteous judgment and justice? That is what God's Kingdom runs on.

This is Difficult for Some

God was the first politician; Jesus was a politician par excellence. When He left for heaven, the Holy Spirit became the Governor for the Kingdom of God on earth. This is a political position. I know you have difficulty with the concept of the

Father, Son, and Holy Spirit being associated with politics. That is because you have a warped understanding of it. Let me remind you of what the Psalmist says: *"For the kingdom is the Lord's: and he is the governor among the nations" (Psalm 22:28)*. What we have done as God's people, just like the Israelites, is that we have allowed the culture of the world, the leaders to inform, interpret, and tell us what the Bible is saying. Jesus put it succinctly: *"And ye have not his word abiding in you: for whom he hath sent, him ye believe not. Search the scriptures; for in them ye think ye have eternal life: and they are they which testify of me. And ye will not come to me, that ye might have life" (John 5:38-40)*. The Word must be in you.

Instead, you have the culture, traditions, men's philosophies, hearsay, regurgitations, our feelings, not the pure Word of God dwelling in us. Hence, what you have is second-hand information. Yes, you read the Bible, but you read it through the eyes of your religion, your belief system. Thus, you read to confirm what you already believe. Yet, like the religious people of Jesus' day, they did not know Him. It is always about the Father, Son, and Holy Spirit—not you or your church, denomination, doctrines, decisions, or directions. Allow the Spirit to inform you.

CHAPTER 8

Biblical Characters Involved in Politics

God and His obedient stewards were and are involved in the political arena. This is repeated over and over in the Bible: *"And he changeth the times and the seasons: he removeth kings, and setteth up kings: he giveth wisdom unto the wise, and knowledge to them that know understanding: He revealeth the deep and secret things: he knoweth what is in the darkness, and the light dwelleth with him. I thank thee, and praise thee, O thou God of my fathers, who hast given me wisdom and might, and hast made known unto me now what we desired of thee: for thou hast now made known unto us the king's matter"* (Daniel 2:21-23). This same prophet further states: *"This matter is by the decree of the watchers, and the demand by the word of the holy ones: to the intent that the living may know that the most High ruleth in the kingdom of men, and giveth it to whomsoever he will, and setteth up over it the basest of men"* (Daniel 4: 17 see also Daniel 4:32, Romans 13). God is always involved in the political process and rightly so. After all, He created it and thus has the right and authority to rule in the affairs of man. With this background in mind, let us examine some biblical characters involved in this field.

Adam and Eve

This was God's instructions when He created them: *"And God blessed them, and God said unto them, Be fruitful, and multiply, and replenish the earth, and subdue it: and have dominion over the fish of the sea, and over the fowl of the air, and over every living thing that moveth upon the earth" (Genesis 1:28).* After creating, He gave them dominion and authority to expand upon what was given to them. How, by using what He gave them, being fruitful, reproducing, and filling the earth, subduing and dominating it. Many make the mistake and limit this to the reproduction of making children. No, it was whatever God gave to them and what He has given us today. We must go through this process. To accomplish this, you must do some conquering. This is what people, politicians, governments, and kingdoms do. Thus, Adam and Eve were the first politicians in God's earthly kingdom (Matthew 25:34). They were placed in Eden to govern the earth.

Noah

The next prominent political leader God called upon to lead His people was Noah. The earth that God created had become very corrupt. Let us read it: *"And God saw that the wickedness of man was great in the earth, and that every imagination of the thoughts of his heart was only evil continually. And it repented the Lord that he had made man on the earth, and it grieved him at his heart. And the Lord said, I will destroy man whom I have created from the face of the earth; both man, and beast, and the creeping thing, and the fowls of the air; for it repenteth me that I have made them. But Noah found grace in the eyes of the Lord" (Genesis 6:5-8).* This was the contrast: Noah recognized the grace of God, and He called upon him to share it with the rest of the then-known world. He was campaigning for God as instructed, unfortunately, the only ones who listened were his family members. Based on our concept of success, we would say He was not a successful politician. Even though your family is the hardest to win over, yet, he managed to win over his entire family. From God's perspective, Noah was successful. He and his family had a similar opportunity to Adam and Eve, a new and fresh start. However, because of the wickedness of man's heart, the same thing continued to happen and is still happening today.

Abraham and Sarah

Let us skip Job, who was also a politician, and go to Abraham and Sarah. As you continue to read Genesis, these were the next politicians God chose. Look at the impact that Abraham and Sarah had and is having on the world: " *Now the Lord had said unto Abram, Get thee out of thy country, and from thy kindred, and from thy father's house, unto a land that I will shew thee: And I will make of thee a great nation, and I will bless thee, and make thy name great; and thou shalt be a blessing: And I will bless them that bless thee, and curse him that curseth thee: and in thee shall all families of the earth be blessed"* (Genesis 12:1-3). They were in charge of the nation to which God was calling them, just like Adam and Eve were. They made some terrible blunders in the process, such as Abraham giving up Sarah to two kings to save his own life. We typically consider Abraham to be the most important in this process. Look at what the Lord did to save Sarah's life on two occasions. One was immediately after the promise you just read: *"And the Lord plagued Pharaoh and his house with great plagues because of Sarai Abram's wife"* (Genesis 12:17). *"But God came to Abimelech in a dream by night, and said to him, Behold, thou art but a dead man, for the woman which thou hast taken; for she is a man's wife. Now therefore restore the man his wife; for he is a prophet, and he shall pray for thee, and thou shalt live: and if thou restore her not, know thou that thou shalt surely die, thou, and all that are thine"*

(Genesis 20:3,7). The Lord is here showing that Sarah played an equal part in this political process, as read in Genesis 17. You will discover that God changed both their names and made them the same promises. Sarah gave him permission to sleep with her maid, creating the conflict that still exists in the Middle East today. Yet, Abraham is the father and Sarah is the mother of all Israel, not just physical Israel, but also spiritual Israel. This is how Paul puts it: *"For he is not a Jew, which is one outwardly; neither is that circumcision, which is outward in the flesh: But he is a Jew, which is one inwardly; and circumcision is that of the heart, in the spirit, and not in the letter; whose praise is not of men, but of God"* (Romans 2:28-29). God called them as the leaders and thus the political leaders of God's people.

Joseph

We cannot name them all, so we will skip some, like Isaac and Jacob, who had a son named Joseph, whom God called to political office outside of Israel. Called to serve in a foreign government, down in Egypt. God will call some of you to serve in the political arena, because He has given you the gift of government *(1 Corinthians 12:28)*. You must understand, like Joseph, that you are called to serve in a foreign government, it is contrary to the government that Jesus came to set up *(Isaiah 9:6-7)*. Just like Jesus, who was called to serve in a foreign government, because this was not the world that He created. Without this understanding, you will never accomplish what God wants from you. It is like Jesus says: *"Jesus answered, My kingdom is not of this world: if my kingdom were of this world, then would my servants fight, that I should not be delivered to the Jews: but now is my kingdom not from hence"* (John 18:36). Joseph understood this very clearly, although it was not immediately apparent. When he was ready, God made him President, second in command to the King of Egypt. He was a great and influential politician who looked out for his people and those of the surrounding nations as a result of the 7 years of famine. The Bible actually says that he helped to save the Israelites from extinction. When God calls you to politics, it is always with the intention to save His people, not always physically, but also spiritually.

Moses

God called Moses one of His next political leaders to lead the Israelites out of Egypt. Like Joseph, he did not initially understand the calling to which God was preparing him. It was different from how the Kingdoms of this world operate. He wanted to lead them out by the military strategy he had learnt and was ready to kill every Egyptian if need be. Instead, God was going to use a foreign method to accomplish this task.

When Moses' method failed, he ran to the desert of Midian and became a shepherd. He went from being the next in line to be the King of Egypt (a politician) to looking after sheep. God was preparing him to be the politician He wanted him to be and lead the Israelites out of Egypt. There is no doubt that Moses was a skilled politician and one of the most effective leaders to guide the Israelites. It is estimated that there were between 1 and 5 million people.

Still do not believe he was a politician. One of the things politicians do is pass laws, right? *"And the Lord said unto Moses, Come up to me into the mount, and be there: and I will give thee tables of stone, and a law, and commandments which I have written; that thou mayest teach them."* (*Exodus 24:12*). Again you read, *"These are the statutes and judgments and laws, which the Lord made between him and the children of Israel in mount Sinai by the hand of Moses"* (*Leviticus 26:46*).

Another thing that politicians deal with is the health of the nation, so did Moses: *"And the leper in whom the plague is, his clothes shall be rent, and his head bare, and he shall put a covering upon his upper lip, and shall cry, Unclean, unclean" (Leviticus 13:45).*

Moses through wisdom, God gave to his father-in-law, Jethro, instructions as to how to set up the judicial system: *"Moreover thou shalt provide out of all the people able men, such as fear God, men of truth, hating covetousness; and place such over them, to be rulers of thousands, and rulers of hundreds, rulers of fifties, and rulers of tens: And let them judge the people at all seasons: and it shall be, that every great matter they shall bring unto thee, but every small matter they shall judge: so shall it be easier for thyself, and they shall bear the burden with thee" (Exodus 18:21-22).* This is still part of the judicial system today and falls under the government's authority. Our concept of politics has been distorted due to the way we have been taught. Thus, we have to unlearn some of the information we were and are given.

Joshua

Then God called upon Joshua, after Moses' death, to be the next political leader of Israel. He was responsible for leading the Israelites into the Canaan: *"Now after the death of Moses the servant of the Lord it came to pass, that the Lord spake unto Joshua the son of Nun, Moses' minister, saying, Moses my servant is dead; now therefore arise, go over this Jordan, thou, and all this people, unto the land which I do give to them, even to the children of Israel. Every place that the sole of your foot shall tread upon, that have I given unto you, as I said unto Moses" (Joshua 1:1-3).*

God then gives him the boundaries for the land of Israel. He talks about dispossessing the other nations. If you are not convinced that this is not politics, then read this: *"There shall not any man be able to stand before thee all the days of thy life: as I was* with Moses, so I will be with thee: I will not fail thee, nor forsake thee. Be strong and of a good courage: for unto this people shalt thou divide for an inheritance the land, which I sware unto their fathers to give them" (Joshua 1:5-6). Is this not what governments do?

Judges

When they got into Canaan, God then instituted the Judicial System, where He uses Judges to be Israel's political leaders: "*Nevertheless, the Lord raised up judges, who delivered them out of the hand of those that spoiled them. And yet they would not hearken unto their judges, but they went a whoring after other gods, and bowed themselves unto them: they turned quickly out of the way which their fathers walked, obeying the commandments of the Lord; but they did not so.... And it came to pass, when the judge was dead, that they returned, and corrupted themselves more than their fathers, following other gods to serve them, and to bow down unto them; they ceased not from their own doings, nor from their stubborn way. And the anger of the Lord was hot against Israel; and he said, because this people hath transgressed my covenant which I commanded their fathers, and have not hearkened unto my voice. I also will not henceforth drive out any from before them of the nations which Joshua left when he died: That through them I may prove Israel, whether they will keep the way of the Lord to walk therein, as their fathers did keep it, or not*" (Judges 2:16-22). As you see, the Judges were the political leaders of Israel. God worked through them.

Kings

There is no doubt that kings and queens are political offices. Israel was not satisfied with the system that God gave them, and so they wanted a king to be like the other nations. This is what they told Samuel the last prophet, who was the political leader of Israel: "*Then all the elders of Israel gathered themselves together, and* came to Samuel unto Ramah, And said unto him, Behold, thou art old, and thy sons walk not in thy ways: now make us a king to judge us like all the nations" (1 Samuel 8:4-5).* This indicates that the prophet Samuel was not only the spiritual leader of Israel but also the political leader. He felt offended because he thought they were rejecting his leadership.

They wanted the same political system the world enjoyed. This was not God's plan for them: *"And the Lord said unto Samuel, Hearken unto the voice of the people in all that they say unto thee: for they have not rejected thee, but they have rejected me, that I should not reign over them" (1 Samuel 8:7).* The Lord warned them that the human-made political system was not in their best interest. In verses 11-19, the Lord iterates the disadvantages of the political system using earthly kings. He said in essence that they will take your sons and use them to run his chariots, as horsemen, and make them captains over thousands. The Kings will make them his farmers, makers of weapons for war. They will make your daughters cooks, bakers, and confectioners. The Kings will take your land and give it to their servants. They will have to pay taxes to cover the King's expenses. You will come back crying to me, but I will not listen to you.

Look at their response: *"Nevertheless, the people refused to obey the voice of Samuel; and they said, Nay; but we will have a king over us" (1 Samuel 8:19).* Of course, this was contrary to the Kingdom of God and hence led to the demise of Israel as a nation. Today, God is using spiritual Israel as a nation to do what physical Israel failed to do.

CHAPTER 9

Women and Politics

By the way, not only were men involved in politics, but women also were. God is not afraid of women being involved politically.

Eve

She was the first woman to enter the political arena. God called her to rule with her husband over the earthly kingdom He created. This was God's plan that the male and female co-rule: *"And God said, Let us make man in our image, after our likeness: and let them have dominion over the fish of the sea, and over the fowl of the air, and over the cattle, and over all the earth, and over every creeping thing that creepeth upon the earth. So God created man in His own image, in the image of God created He him; male and female created He them. And God blessed them, and God said unto them, Be fruitful, and multiply, and replenish the earth, and subdue it: and have dominion over the fish of the sea, and over the fowl of the air, and over every living thing that moveth upon the earth"* (Genesis 1:26-28). That is what she did; this partnership has not ended. He still wants males and females to rule together, not one over the other.

Sarah

She was called upon to co-rule with her husband. Let us see how much she was involved in Israel's politics: *"And God said unto Abraham, As for Sarai thy wife, thou shalt not call her name Sarai, but Sarah shall her name be. And I will bless her, and give thee a son also of her: yea, I will bless her, and she shall be a mother of nations; kings of people shall be of her" (Genesis 17:15-17)*. If you read verses 5-8, you will discover that it is the same promise given to Abraham. He changed their names. She was the mother and king of nations, and Abraham was the father and king of nations; they both held political positions. God's plan was, and always is, for us to co-rule with Him and with each other. Not just the males, but females are also ruling this earth together. That is why, in the Bible, God makes both male and female Kings: *"And from Jesus Christ, who is the faithful witness, and the first begotten of the dead, and the prince of the kings of the earth. Unto him that loved us, and washed us from our sins in his own blood, and hath made us kings and priests unto God and his Father; to him be glory and dominion forever. Amen (Revelation 1:5-6)*. There are only two ways to become a king: the first is by lineage or blood. The second is usurping the throne, that is, taking it by force. Well, the latter cannot happen in God's jurisdiction. He made us kings through His blood. Notice the tense is not future, but past; it is already done. To make sure that we get it John, the Revelator records it twice: *"And they sung a new song, saying, Thou art worthy to take the book, and to open the seals thereof: for thou wast slain, and hast redeemed us to God by thy blood out of every kindred, and tongue, and people, and nation; And hast made us unto our God kings and priests: and we shall reign on the earth" (Revelation 5:9-10)*. He is basically repeating the same in the previous verses. Notice also that it is not restricted to males; the Lord includes both sexes, because in God's economy, there are no queens; all are kings—a powerful demonstration of equality. I was teaching this concept at a church, and a lady in the congregation was adamant because I said we are all kings, not queens; to me, it is saying equality. I understood where she was coming from. Can't we, as women, get our own identity? Well, it is not ours, it is God's.

Deborah

She was an outstanding woman who was a prophetess, judge, and Israel's political leader. One of Israel's forms of government, as we established, was Judges appointed by God, who were the political rulers in Israel at the time. This is what happened: *"And the children of Israel again did evil in the sight of the Lord, when Ehud was dead. And the Lord sold them into the hand of Jabin, king of Canaan, that reigned in Hazor; the captain of whose host was Sisera, who dwelt in Harosheth of the Gentiles. And the children of Israel cried unto the Lord: for he had nine hundred chariots of iron; and twenty years he mightily oppressed the children of Israel. And Deborah, a prophetess, the wife of Lapidoth, she judged Israel at that time. And she dwelt under the palm tree of Deborah between Ramah and Bethel in mount Ephraim: and the children of Israel came up to her for judgment"* (Judges 4:1-5). As can be seen, she wore several hats; she was the spiritual, judicial, and political leader of Israel. The spiritual leader was straightforward; she was a prophetess. The judicial system is obvious, she judged the Israelites. How do we know she was the political leader? Because, like a king, she would judge the children of Israel. Just like King David and his son Solomon did. Here is further proof she was their political leader in addition to judging, she was also over the military: *"And she sent and called Barak the son of Abinoam out of Kedeshnaphtali, and said unto him, Hath not the Lord God of Israel commanded, saying, Go and draw toward mount Tabor, and take with thee ten thousand men of the children of Naphtali and of the children of Zebulun? And I will draw unto thee to the river Kishon Sisera, the captain of Jabin's army, with his chariots and his multitude; and I will deliver him into thine hand."* Barak was the commander of Israel's army, and she gave him the instructions that God gave her to give to him. There was such great respect for Deborah, here is what he said to her: *"And Barak said unto her, If thou wilt go with me, then I will go: but if thou wilt not go with me, then I will not go. And she said, I will surely go with thee: notwithstanding the journey that thou takest shall not be for thine honour; for the Lord shall sell Sisera into the hand of a woman. And Deborah arose, and went with Barak to Kedesh"* (Judges 4:6-9).

Barak was a strong and powerful man of God who was not intimidated by women. He solicited her help; he was not going to battle if Deborah was not going with him—the first recorded woman in the Bible who went into combat for her country. Furthermore, Barak was not troubled that a woman would get the credit for killing Sisera, the Commander, who was the head of the King of Canaan's army. Let us read what happened: *"Howbeit Sisera fled away on his feet to the tent of Jael, the wife of Heber the Kenite: for there was peace between Jabin the king of Hazor and the house of Heber the Kenite. And Jael went out to meet Sisera, and said unto him, Turn in, my lord, turn in to me; fear not. And when he had turned in unto her into the tent, she covered him with a mantle. And he said unto her, Give me, I pray thee, a little water to drink; for I am thirsty. And she opened a bottle of milk and gave it to him to drink, then covered him. Again, he said unto her, stand in the door of the tent, and it shall be, when any man doth come and enquire of thee, and say, Is there any man here? That thou shalt say, No. Then Jael Heber's wife took a nail of the tent, and took a hammer in her hand, and went softly unto him, and smote the nail into his temples, and fastened it into the ground: for he was fast asleep and weary. So he died. And, behold, as Barak pursued Sisera, Jael came out to meet him, and said unto him, Come, and I will shew thee the man whom thou seekest.*

And when he came into her tent, behold, Sisera lay dead, and the nail was in his temples. So God subdued on that day Jabin, the king of Canaan, before the children of Israel. And the hand of the children of Israel prospered, and prevailed against Jabin the king of Canaan, until they had destroyed Jabin king of Canaan" (Judges 4:17-24). Jael was another woman who went to war for her country as well.

Like Barak, we should not be afraid as men when God calls women to carry out the tasks He assigned them. Instead, we should support them because in the end, the goal is accomplished, and all Israel benefited from Barak listening to God through Deborah.

Esther

When Israel found itself in serious trouble in Persia, there was a plot to destroy the Israelites. God raised up Queen Esther in a foreign kingdom to become the Queen of Persia, thereby saving His people. Again, this is a political position, and as you will see, she was able to influence the Kingdom of Persia and save the children of Israel from annihilation. I love the way that Mordacai puts it: *"For if thou altogether holdest thy peace at this time, then shall their enlargement and deliverance arise to the Jews from another place; but thou and thy father's house shall be destroyed: and who knoweth whether thou art come to the kingdom for such a time as this?"* (Esther 4:14). He was saying in essence, this is your moment, you have come to the Kingdom for this opportunity. If you don't make use of it, God will use someone else to deliver His people, because we will be delivered. Understanding this, she stepped up to the plate. With the help of the Holy Spirit, we need discernment to know when the women in our lives who have come to the Kingdom of God for their moment, and to support them in the process.

Athahliah

Now, some of you will have difficulty with this one. God allowed Athaliah to be the queen of Israel. He disagreed with her method of becoming the political leader of Judah. Here is how the Bible describes it: *"And when Athaliah the mother of Ahaziah saw that her son was dead, she arose and destroyed all the seed royal"* (2 Kings 11:1). When she learnt her son, Ahaziah (AKA Azariah or Jehoahaz), was dead, she murdered all her sons and grandchildren so that she could become the political leader of Judah, queen. The Bible states that she ruled for six years *(2 Kings 11:3)*.

Because of our culture with women being subservient to men, very seldom do you hear about Athaliah ruling as a queen over Judah.

Women Financed Jesus' Ministry

In Jesus' government that He came to set up, where did the money come from to fund His ministries? *"After this, Jesus traveled about from one town and village to another, proclaiming the good news of the kingdom of God. The Twelve were with him, and also some women who had been cured of evil spirits and diseases: Mary (called Magdalene), from whom seven demons had come out; Joanna, the wife of Chuza, the manager of Herod's household; Susanna; and many others. These women were helping to support them out of their own means"* (Luke 8:1-3). Every time I read this, it fills my soul with joy. When I was growing up, you didn't take money from women. It was the opposite. This was politically incorrect according to Man, but to God, no problem. Thus, these women played a crucial role in advancing Jesus' kingdom agenda. Furthermore, we typically say that Jesus had only 12 male disciples, as evidenced here; not only were they women of means who were His disciples, but the Bible also mentions that many other women followed Him. As Elder Francis pointed out, there were more women following

Jesus than men, and I agree that this is a situation similar to the current one.

Should Disciples Be Involved Politically

Yes, because the Bible is a political book. God is involved and has always been involved in politics. Furthermore, politics originated with God, not humanity. It is impossible to be alive and escape politics; this is not limited to males; it also affects all females. I know that this creates dissonance for some of us. This is my understanding. I pray for wisdom and that this book will spark your curiosity, inspiring you to delve deeper into this vital subject. Once there is more than one person, there must be rules, regulations, policies, and a political system to live in peace and harmony.

Your Fight Daily Is Political

Do you know that the fight you are in is a political one? Again, this is not limited to gender. Do you know you have to vote every morning when you open your eyes, as to who you will allow to be in charge of your life for the following x number of hours you are awake? Who are you voting for when you wake up? You always have to choose, because that is the greatest essence of life, making choices. It is such a great reality that if you do not choose, you choose by default. Just as it happens in politics, you are allowed to vote for the candidate you want to run your life and country for the next x number of years. Who do you want to decide your standard of living, morals, laws, and regulations that govern your life and country? You have to determine who will run your life every day. And you only have two choices; everything you do and say in life is contingent on one of those choices. The Apostle Paul breaks it down as we read in *Romans 6:16*.

I know this is not politically correct, but as the Apostle Paul says, we are all slaves. The good news is you get to choose who your master is. Why are you a slave? Every created being is subject to their Creator. It does not matter whether you like it or not. Whatever you invent or create is subject to you; that makes sense because you are the one who created it. It cannot tell you what to do. It is like your children, when they are young, you are in charge of them. They don't tell you what to do; you tell them. I know I am going to get in trouble for this, but they are your slaves. How you treat them is what makes the difference. Because of love, you treat them with dignity and respect and look out for their best interests. That is what God does for you, His faithful steward. If you make the enemy your master, as John the beloved points out, he comes to kill, steal, and destroy *(John 10:10)*.

CHAPTER 10

The Bible is God's Manifesto and Constitution

It would be beneficial to follow God's Biblical instructions. It is a political book. It is God's Manifesto and Constitution. Do you know that when they fought in the Old Testament, it was over whose god was the most powerful?

Definition of Manifesto and Constitution

A manifesto is: "A written statement that describes the policies, goals, and opinions of a person or group. A written statement declaring publicly the intentions, motives, or views of its issuer" (Merriam-Webster Dictionary). Thus, the Bible is God's Manifesto. It declares publicly who the Father, Son, and Holy Spirit are and their intentions, views, and what they think of us.

A constitution, on the other hand, is the basic principles and laws of a nation, state, or social group that determine the powers and duties of the government and guarantee certain rights to the people in it—a written instrument embodying the rules of a political or social organization (Merriam-Webster Dictionary). The Bible is also God's constitution; it contains the principles, values, laws, commandments, and our rights.

There are also consequences for not following the constitution; these can be both ethical and legal, and one may face criminal charges or be subject to censorship. These measures are taken to maintain accountability and ensure that the laws outlined in the Constitution are upheld. All of these are found in God's constitution, the Bible.

Proof The Bible Is God's Manifesto & Constitution

Here is a perfect example of what the Bible is. This is just one chapter of the manifesto and constitution. Moses declares: *"And it shall come to pass, when all these things are come upon thee, the blessing and the curse, which I have set before thee, and thou shalt call them to mind among all the nations, whither the LORD thy God hath driven thee, And shalt return unto the LORD thy God, and shalt obey his voice according to all that I command thee this day, thou and thy children, with all thine heart, and with all thy soul; That then the LORD thy God will turn thy captivity, and have compassion upon thee, and will return and gather thee from all the nations, whither the LORD thy God hath scattered thee"* (Deuteronomy 30:1-3). God is here declaring publicly His intentions, policies, goals, instructions, views, laws, rules, regulations, expectations, and opinions to the Israelites. If the children believe what God said in His manifesto and constitution, and they love the Lord with all their heart, mind, and soul, obey His voice, and carry out all His commands. He promised to bring them and us back from all parts of the earth.

Benefits

These are the benefits God will give if you follow His manifesto and constitution:

Abundance

"And the LORD thy God will bring thee into the land which thy fathers possessed, and thou shalt possess it; and he will do thee good, and multiply thee above thy fathers....And the LORD thy God will make thee plenteous in every work of thine hand, in the fruit of thy body, cattle, and land, for good: for the LORD will again rejoice over thee for good, as he rejoiced over thy fathers (Deuteronomy 30:5, 9). **You will have more than your fathers, and will multiply in all areas, that is His promise to His stewards.**

Heart Circumcision

"And the LORD thy God will circumcise thine heart, and the heart of thy seed, to love the LORD thy God with all thine heart, and with all thy soul, that thou mayest live" (Deuteronomy 30:6). This living He is talking about is not mere existence; this is living life to its fullest and enjoying the Lord, your family, friends, church members, neighbors, and co-workers and being able to love them genuinely, with all your heart, mind, and soul. It is life at another level, higher than you have ever experienced.

Curse Your Enemies

"And the LORD thy God will put all these curses upon thine enemies, and on them that hate thee, which persecuted thee" (Deuteronomy 30:7). That is one of the reasons you can enjoy life because you don't have to worry about your enemies; the Lord will take care of them. However, it is about following His policies, as outlined in His Manifesto and Constitution. And this is what it says: "And thou shalt return and obey the voice of the LORD, and do all his commandments which I command thee this day. If thou shalt hearken unto the voice of the LORD thy God, to keep his commandments and his statutes which are written in this book of the law, and if thou turn unto the LORD thy God with all thine heart, and with all thy soul" (Deuteronomy 30:8-10).

As you notice, it is a heart, not a head thing; it is not physical, but spiritual; it is not about dos and don'ts, but about fellowship and becoming intimate with the Father, Son, and Holy Spirit.

We are Given Choice

You always have a choice, that is what His Manifesto and Constitution are about: *"See, I have set before thee this day life and good, and death and evil; In that I command thee this day to love the LORD thy God, to walk in his ways, and to keep his commandments and his statutes and his judgments, that thou mayest live and multiply: and the LORD thy God shall bless thee in the land whither thou goest to possess it" (Deuteronomy 30:15-16).* If you choose the way of the manifesto and constitution, to love the Lord your God and respond to His instructions, you will live abundantly, everyone and everything you have will multiply. You will be protected wherever God sends you, and you will be safe; nobody can harm you unless He permits it. When He does, He has already equipped you with what it takes to handle that situation. Remember, it is always political. Who are you voting for daily?

What Choices Are You Making?

There are consequences for choices you make: *"But if thine heart turn away, so that thou wilt not hear, but shalt be drawn away, and worship other gods, and serve them; I denounce unto you this day, that ye shall surely perish, and that ye shall not prolong your days upon the land, whither thou passest over Jordan to go to possess it. I call heaven and earth to record this day against you, that I have set before you life and death, blessing and cursing: therefore choose life, that both thou and thy seed may live: That thou mayest love the LORD thy God, and that thou mayest obey his voice, and mayest cleave unto him: for he is thy life, and the length of thy days: that thou mayest dwell in the land which the LORD sware unto thy fathers, to Abraham,*

Isaac, Jacob, to give them" (Deuteronomy 30:17-20). Did you notice that it comes back to the heart again? It is about loving God, and this love will motivate you to be obedient, kind, gentle, long-suffering, ready to forgive and love.

Jesus Shows the Bible Is God's Manifesto

Another clear indication that the Bible is God's Manifesto and Constitution is the Sermon on the Mount. It builds on the Old Testament, and if you compare it to Deuteronomy 30, you will discover that it is essentially a repetition. It shows us how to live in God's Kingdom. Let us examine some verses from a single chapter from the Sermon on the Mount and see God's Manifesto. We will look at the Constitution and its impact on those who ignore its instructions: *"And seeing the multitudes, he went up into a mountain: and when he was set, his disciples came unto him: And he opened his mouth, and taught them, saying, Blessed are the poor in spirit: for theirs is the kingdom of heaven. Blessed are they that mourn: for they shall be comforted. Blessed are the meek: for they shall inherit the earth. Blessed are they who hunger and thirst after righteousness, for they shall be filled. Blessed are the merciful, for they shall obtain mercy. Blessed are the pure in heart, for they shall see God. Blessed are the peacemakers, for they shall be called the children of God. Blessed are they who are persecuted for righteousness' sake: for theirs is the kingdom of heaven. Blessed are ye, when men shall revile you, and persecute you, and shall say all manner of evil against you falsely, for my sake. Rejoice, and be exceeding glad: for great is your reward in heaven: for so persecuted they the prophets which were before you"* (Matthew 5:1-12). The big difference is that Jesus takes it to the next level, and that is where He now wants you to operate. Remember, once you accept Jesus as your personal Savior, you become a spiritual being, so you begin to operate from a higher perspective. Until you do that, you will not understand what Jesus or His Word is saying to you *(1 Corinthians 2:14)*.

Now let us look at the Bible as God's constitution: *"Ye have heard that it was said of them of old time, Thou shalt not kill; and whosoever shall kill shall be in danger of the judgment: But I say unto you, That whosoever is angry with his brother without a cause shall be in danger of the judgment: and whosoever shall say to his brother, Raca, shall be in danger of the council: but whosoever shall say, Thou fool, shall be in danger of hell fire" (Matthew 5:21-22)*. Here, you see the Lord laying down the consequences for our actions.

God's Kingdom is Different

Remember what Jesus said to His disciples in John 18:36 that His Kingdom, His ways, are diametrically opposed to those of the world. It is contrary to the world, and so what man says and does, if they are not converted, then almost everything they say, you must do the opposite. Remember what you just read about what the Prophet Isaiah said in Chapter 55 of his book. Herein lies the greatest danger, what the enemy loves to do best, and that is to deceive. His deception is very subtle. Recall his encounter with Eve in the Garden of Eden? The same principles that were necessary to run God's government are also required to run His Kingdom government today. All our gifts, purposes, ministries, vocations, and destiny are needed for the success of His government. It cannot be about the individual; it must be about our community, our country, or else, as with the Jews rebuilding Jerusalem, Nehemiah had to rebuke the rich who were taking advantage of the poor *(Nehemiah 5)*. Are you trying to serve people or take advantage of them? Then you are not following God's Manifesto and will suffer the consequences for not following His Constitution.

CHAPTER 11

My Experience in Politics

You may have heard or read about this story when I visited my country in December of 2013. My purpose was to launch my Dad's Autobiography, which we had published. While there, a young man was shot, not sure of his age, left behind a little daughter, who was less than two years old.

I had just read on the plane in one of American Airlines' Periodicals that there is a church for every mile in my country, Anguilla. Now, there are two churches for every mile. When I heard the news, I was furious and wanted to know, given the numerous churches on the island, what they were doing to make a positive impact and difference in our country. I know that most churches in our denomination are not doing as much as they should. Yes, we are making an impact internationally through our organization, the Adventist Development and Relief Agency. However, locally, we are not doing much. It was then the Spirit convicted me. You are asking what the churches are doing? Let me ask you, what are you doing? I said, "Okay, Lord, I am willing and available to be used by you, however you see fit." You must be very careful about how and for what you pray.

Immediately, the Lord opened the door for me to appear on the Mayor's Show, a political broadcast that deals with national problems and finding solutions. Here is how the Lord confirmed to me that this is where He wanted me to be. The Honorable Palmovan Webster, who was responsible for ensuring my dad's book got published, was in her office. My brother Frankie and I went to thank her for her generosity. She asked me, "What about coming on the Mayor's Show tomorrow and giving away 10 of his books? I will pay for them." Then she remembered it was Friday and the next day was the Sabbath, and I go to church on Saturday, and said Oh, I forgot. I whispered a prayer, and the Spirit impressed upon me, Go. I then said to her, I will be there. Whenever God asks me to do something, I always look for confirmation to make sure it was Him and not me.

I compiled 10 questions from the book that the public had to answer to receive a copy. This was the Mayor's Show annual giveaway in honor of the one who started the program, Mr. Yanchie Richardson, aka the Mayor's, birthday. I went to the station, and they allowed me to ask my questions. In less than 30 minutes, I was finished, and I sat there and listened.

I began to question God. Why did I have to come to the station? I could have given them the questions, and they could have given away the books. Let me rewind a bit. Whenever I visit any country, I contact the Adventist ministers and inquire about their needs while I am there to see if I can help to fulfill some of them. I called the Pastor on Wednesday and did not get him. I left a message, and he did not return my call. While I was sitting there, Conrad Rogers was in the studio, but Yanchie Richardson, also known as the Mayor, and Tyrone Hodge were calling from the United States, and they were on the phone for over two hours. I was trying to figure out how they did that; it must cost a fortune. Then, as the program was about to end, I was still questioning God when the program's producer, Leroy Richardson, also known as Bro Lee, asked me, "Are you coming in to do your broadcast tomorrow live?" At the time, I was sending in recordings for my program, the Kingdom Agenda Broadcast. I had visited home on several occasions, and it never even occurred to me to go in and do it live.

What made the confirmation even more powerful is that the producer for my program, Monique Webster, was in the studio and heard it. And thus, it was arranged. I went into the studio and it was a wonderful experience. Just as I was finished with the broadcast and went in to thank my producer, the idea of how they were able to call for two hours on the phone from America still hadn't been calculated, and I was trying to figure out the cost. While I am thinking this, Sis Monique, my producer from my program, said to me, "I have a magic jack and I could bring it and download it so that you can have a live broadcast from Houston, Texas." She could not have known that that was what I was thinking. I did not share it with anyone. This was additional confirmation, I could do the same as them live on my program as well. Here is some more: if the Pastor had answered me and needed me to preach or teach, then I would have left and missed these golden opportunities. The Mayor immediately saw my potential and invited me to return to the broadcast the very next week, and I have been on for almost 12 years now.

The Election of A Woman

I believe in the Gospel Commission that Jesus gave before leaving the earth. He said, 'Go ye into all the world and preach the gospel' (Matthew 28:19). This is a command from God that the church has narrowed to certain places and people. We have ignored for too long most of the political arena, and I now have a better understanding of what Jesus meant. You see, I just returned from my country (Anguilla), where general elections were held on 22 April 2015. I had the privilege of being part of the process.

I want to thank the Honorable Palmavon Webster of District 1, Yanchie Richardson, also known as The Mayor, Tyronne Hodge, and Conrad Rogers, the panelists, and Leroy Richardson, the Producer, for allowing me to be a part of that process.

General elections are a significant issue in my country, and I was invited to contribute on the radio and on a political platform. It was an amazing and rewarding experience. I had the opportunity to interact with my fellow country people, listen to their pain, wants, needs, hopes, aspirations, and dreams. I gained a clearer understanding of some of our roles as Kingdom stewards in the political arena.

Mission Trip

Before leaving for my country on the last of three different trips for the elections, the Spirit impressed upon me that I am sending you on a mission trip. I didn't quite get it, because you don't typically go to your own country on a mission trip, at least that is what I was taught. Now I know, yes, people do go to their homeland on mission trips. That is what the Lord does sometimes: He does not give you the details. However, He will reveal to you when it is happening or after it has happened. I had the privilege of hanging out with Yanchie, the Mayor. Normally, when I go home, I hang out with my parents. I try to spend as much time as possible with them. Well, it is only my mother who is alive, and there was a greater need to spend time with her, because she lost her husband of 60 years. Yet, the Lord had another agenda for me, and my mother understood.

Go Ye Into All The World

Too often, we want the people to come. But, to accomplish this, as Jesus said, I had to go where they were. Before and after elections, the Mayor and I would go to the bars, restaurants, and homes—into their backyards, to their barbeques. This was not for political purposes; this was just for fellowship. True, there are some things they were doing that I would not do, but Jesus said Go ye into all the world, this was a part of the world, and what an experience. I will never forget, while returning to the courthouse where the ballot counting was taking place, that The Honorable Evalie Bradley, after winning her seat, was standing in the parking lot when the Mayor gathered her and her supporters who were accompanying her. He asked me to pray for them. That was a humbling and incredible experience.

Praying On One

Then, on the next night, we went to Blowing Point, where the AUF Party was celebrating. They were grilling and drinking, having a great time. The Mayor introduced me to the Honorable Curtis Richardson, who won his seat, and I had the opportunity to pray with him one-on-one. The Chief Minister, Victor Banks, joined them later, and Yanchie pulled him aside and asked me to pray for and with him as well. I also prayed for the Honorable Palmavon Webster on several occasions before and after the elections. Then I understood what the Lord meant when He told me I was going on a mission trip.

I was talking to a family friend, Anisha Archibald, and she said that is what Jesus did: He went to where the people were. There are some so-called Christians who would not be found dead in these places, as if they are better than Jesus.

Being Able to Minister

It was a phenomenal experience. After the new Government was sworn in at Ronald Webster Park, Yanchie was looking for a place for us to get a drink, and there was a Chinese Bar that was open. So, we went in, and I had a malt (non-alcoholic beverage). Yanchie had his usual, and I had the privilege of dialoguing with some young men, and what an experience that was. I listened to them and what they had to say, and they listened to me in return.

The Mayor's Show

Now, almost every Sabbath morning, before I go to church, I have the privilege of preaching and teaching my fellow Anguillans and other listeners from the Word of God. The Mayor, the founder of the show, has the gift of discernment. He sees the potential in others and has given me autonomy to take the broadcast in the direction that I believe the Lord is leading me. It reached the point where Klass FM, another station on the Island, also used me to do political commentary on what is happening on the Island. I call a meeting every Friday for the program, so we're all on the same page when we go on the air on Sabbaths. One of the staples on the broadcast now is prayer for our country, those who have lost loved ones, our leaders, family, and any other pertinent prayer requests.

What is Expected

As an obedient steward of Jesus, you must be aware of what is happening in the world, try to understand it, and allow the Spirit to interpret it in the context of His Kingdom. The ideal steward wants to influence the world for Jesus, but you are doomed to be ineffective if you are ignorant.

One of the most difficult and vital lessons the obedient steward of God needs to learn is for the Spirit to reveal any and every kind of discrimination and give you discernment and wisdom in how to handle them. This ability to sort out experiences and choose priorities never comes easily. Perhaps this is why churchgoers often prefer to avoid certain places and issues. It is easier to ignore them; thus, we may never hear from God if He wants us to address the specific problems or go to certain places to help our fellow humans.

The Problem

Why are many of God's people having a hard time with politics? Jesus Himself gives the answer in Mark 12:24: *"And Jesus answering said unto them, Do ye not therefore err, because ye know not the Scriptures, neither the power of God?"* Be aware that Jesus did not say 'your teacher, pastor, parents, husband, or wife. He says, the reason why you err, that is, go astray, sin, come short, make mistakes, slip up, is because you don't know what the Word of God says. Now, if you don't know what the Scriptures say, then you will never fully understand the power of God, nor can you experience it. Because the Word is about God, who He is, and what He is capable of. It is His Manifesto and Constitution.

The Apostle Paul puts it this way: *"Now the Lord is that Spirit: and where the Spirit of the Lord is, there is liberty. But we all, with open face beholding as in a glass the glory of the Lord, are changed into the same image from glory to glory, even as by the Spirit of the Lord"* (2 Corinthians 3:17-18). Not only are you free, you are changed from glory to glory by beholding Him. Where can you find Him to look into His face, in His Word?

What is happening is that you are listening to what people tell you about what is in the Bible, what the Word of God is saying about how you should live your life. No one can do that for you, because God relates to each of His children differently, since that is how He made you. You are unique, so you must hear from God personally. Similarly, smart parents do not parent each child the same way. Too many people are reflectors of other men's thoughts. Thinking is a rare skill; if it is not practiced, it can become a tricky proposition. Unfortunately, you have been taught by society that it is easier to listen to others telling you what to do, rather than reading the Word and listening to the Spirit guiding you. We listen to our parents, teachers, preachers, and politicians and don't normally question what we are hearing.

This is done very early in life, unless the child is strong-willed. As you grow older, you buy into the lie that if it is written in a book, then it must be true. What further complicates this process is that if someone comes along and tells you this is what the book is saying, you accept it, it must be right, because he or she has a Master's, PhD, is a CEO, Lawyer, President, so they must know what they are talking about.

Regrettably, the most gullible are often those who are religious. You can be easily manipulated because you believe that if someone claims to be religious and adds "minister," "bishop," or "priest" to their name, then they can be trusted. What seems to make it even more authentic is if they have attended seminary and have a degree or two behind their names, then they must be holy, genuine, and know God personally; thus, whatever they say must be true.

That is why I love the Bereans, here is what the Bible says about them: *"These were more noble than those in Thessalonica, in that they received the word with all readiness of mind, and searched the Scriptures daily, whether those things were so"* (Acts 17:11). As prominent as the Apostle Paul was, the brethren from Berea, listened eagerly. Yet, they searched the Word for themselves to find out if these things were true. That is what God expects of you, His obedient steward. Don't disappoint Him. If He called you to be a politician, respond to His call, and you will make significant differences. If you have been blessed, please share this information with others and help us change, and, in turn, help others change their concept of politics.

Appendix 1
HOW TO BECOME JESUS' DISCIPLE?

Becoming a disciple is one of the easiest things in the world, as easy as **ABC**. However, it is tough to maintain. The biggest obstacle is its simplicity. It is a three-step process:

A—*"All have sinned and fallen short of the glory of God" (Romans 3:23); and "the wages of sin is death" (Romans 6:23).*

B—*"Behold the Lamb of God who takes away the sins of the world" (John 1:29).*

C—*"Come unto me all who are weary and heavy-burdened and I will give you rest" (Matthew 11:28).*

There is no exception. We all have sinned, the Greek says, "All have sinned and are coming short of the glory of God." It doesn't happen just once, but repeatedly.

Accept this fact, **B**elieve that there is only One sinless being that can save you, and His name is Jesus. Then, **C**onfess by praying the prayer of forgiveness and acknowledgement of who Jesus is to you. Or you can sincerely repeat this prayer:

"Lord Jesus, I have sinned against heaven and against you, and I am sorry. Please forgive me of all my sins. Come into my heart and live as Lord and Savior of my life. Amen."

CONGRATULATIONS, YOU ARE NOW A DISCIPLE OF JESUS

I don't feel any different.

You don't have to: "For it is by grace you have been saved, through faith—and this not from yourselves, it is the gift of God not by works, so that no one can boast" (Ephesians 2:8-9).

How do I live now?

"For in the gospel a righteousness from God is revealed, a righteousness that is by faith from first to last, just as it is written: "The righteous will live by faith" (Romans 1:17).

What happens if I sin again?

"If we confess our sins, he is faithful and just and will forgive us our sins, and purify us from all unrighteousness" (1 John 1:9).

Why should I believe this promise God made?

"God is not a man, that he should lie, nor a son of man, that he should change his mind. Does He speak and then not act? Does he promise and not fulfill?" (Numbers 23:19).

What do I do next?

Pray and ask God to lead you to a church that will disciple you and then teach you how to make disciples. After that, He will help you find your God-given gifts, purposes, ministries, vocations, and destiny. Use these to meet the needs of the people He places in your life to build up His Kingdom. This will produce congruency within, and you will not feel miserable as His Disciple.

Made in the USA
Middletown, DE
06 December 2025